Christianity W...

To Barbara
my good
good
friend
John
11/29/12

CHRISTIANITY
WITHOUT SUPERSTITION

Meaning, Metaphor, and Mystery

JOHN McQUISTON II

Morehouse Publishing
NEW YORK · HARRISBURG · DENVER

Morehouse Publishing, 4775 Linglestown Road, Harrisburg, PA 17112

Morehouse Publishing, 445 Fifth Avenue, New York, NY 10016

Morehouse Publishing is an imprint of Church Publishing Incorporated.
www.churchpublishing.org

Cover design by Laurie Klein Westhafer
Typeset by Vicki K. Black

Library of Congress Cataloging-in-Publication Data
McQuiston, John.
  Christianity without superstition : meaning, metaphor, and mystery / John McQuiston II.
      p.   cm.
Includes bibliographical references.
ISBN 978-0-8192-2738-6 (pbk.) -- ISBN 978-0-8192-2740-9 (ebook)
1. Christianity--Essence, genius, nature. I. Title.
BT60.M38 2012
230--dc23   2012020803

Printed in the United States of America

*This is the ultimate in human knowledge of God:
to know that we do not know Him.*

                ~ Saint Thomas Aquinas,
           Quaestiones Disputatae de Potentia Dei

*I've seen pretty clear, ever since I was a young un, as
religion's something else besides notions.*

              ~ Adam Bede, speaking in
               George Eliot's 1859 novel
                   of the same name

*For my thoughts are not your thoughts,
    neither are your ways my ways, says the LORD.
For as the heavens are higher than the earth,
    so are my ways higher than your ways
    and my thoughts than your thoughts.*

                     ~ Isaiah 55:8–9

Contents

Preface

A friend learned that I was working on a book and asked me for the title. When I said it was *Christianity Without Superstition,* she immediately replied, "That's impossible."

My friend was reflecting a uniquely Western development—the loss of the mythos that once oriented us in the universe. For centuries that mythos was that we are children of an omnipotent creator God, a God with human characteristics, a Father who loves us and sent his son to assure us of life with him, in heaven, after death. Millions today do not believe these images.

Today our culture offers another *mythos*—that we are completely material, finite beings located on an insignificant planet, in a mechanistic, purposeless universe. Very few of us accept this, but in the West it may seem that the choice is between these two visions.

This is a particularly Western dilemma because the images central to the traditional Western *mythos* have often been presented as factual truth, a picture of what actually *is*, not as symbols pointing to the profound mystery of reality.

This book discusses a third alternative.

Should Belief Have Primacy?

For decades I struggled with the question: What should I believe? In that regard I am not unusual. I am a child of Western culture and institutional Christianity. Both have been obsessed with this question for centuries.

People from every background have grappled with this issue and continue to do so, particularly when it appears in the form of the question: "Is there a God?" Richard Dawkins, in *The God Delusion,* says no and Karen Armstrong, in *The Case for God,* says yes. These are but two examples of a debate that began when humans first looked at the stars and wondered. Mankind's ceaseless effort to understand the universe is an expression of the need to know what to believe.

Throughout history, the institutional Christian church has attempted to tell people what they should believe. Declarations of required belief have been put forward in many forms: in sermons, creeds, catechisms, decrees, papal letters, articles of faith, and books of all sorts. Like so many others brought up in a Christian church and a predominately Christian community, I questioned the truth of such statements in my late teens and to a greater extent in college. In this also I am not unusual.

During my second year in law school, my wife and I began to attend a Sunday school class for people who might be interested in joining the Episcopal Church. In that class, I asked the rector of the church what I was required to believe to be a member of this church. I was surprised by his answer: "That is up to you."

At the time I wondered how he could give that answer and not be in conflict with the creeds printed in the *Book of Common Prayer,* as well as in trouble with church authorities. Many years have passed. Today when I recall that answer I think how wise it was.

I live in the United States, in the South, in the heart of the Bible belt. In my city most of the people are church members. But the South is an anomaly. In the United States and Europe huge numbers have rejected Christianity because they do not believe the things Christianity seems to require.

Should being a Christian require belief in the Nicene Creed? The Apostles' Creed? The Catholic Catechism? None of these were written until long after the death of Jesus of Nazareth and his disciples.

A careful study of what Jesus said and did shows that his intended legacy was not a creed but a practice—a *way* of living, a way of relating to one another and the world.

From scriptures that were already ancient in his time, he distilled and taught, by word and example, an extraordinary, life-enhancing method of enriching this life. Jesus showed no interest in authoring any creed or any statement of belief at all.

When Jesus was asked how to find the "kingdom of God," his answer, given centuries before the sciences of psychology and psychiatry, was that the kingdom is found through the creation of an interior state:

> *Once Jesus was asked by the Pharisees when the kingdom of God was coming, and he answered, "The kingdom of God is not coming with things that can be observed; nor will they say, 'Look, here it is!' or 'There it is!' For, in fact, the kingdom of God is within you."*
> ∼ Luke 17:20–22

The Christianity that is the subject of this book does not try to persuade the reader to accept or reject the traditional statements of Christian belief. Although this book is primarily addressed to those who do not believe in the literal truth of the traditional statements of belief, it has no quarrel with those who accept them and the images of the world and God embedded in them.

We might expect that a Christianity that does not require belief that the creeds are statements of fact would have no room for the miraculous and would be reduced to mere secular morality, but it is not, although it is moral, even moral in the extreme. Far from dismissing the miraculous, this Christianity without superstition recognizes that there is a depth to reality beyond our comprehension, a hidden profundity to existence that is suggested by the equations of contemporary physics and the discoveries of science as well as by cathedrals, liturgies, religious art, and music. This Christianity does not insist that we believe that Jesus rose bodily from the dead, but it does ask us to become fully conscious that we, and all living beings, inexplicably arose from the dead, inert detritus of exploded stars. It asks us to become aware that we live in a ceaseless miracle that is ultimately unfathomable. It asks us to wake up to the incredible everyday fact that in this corner of infinite space choirs sing and dirt becomes a living rose. As the old prayer says, "Days pass and years vanish, and we walk sightless among miracles."[1]

A Christianity freed of the demand that we believe things we cannot believe recognizes that this dimensionless universe in which "we live and move and have our being" (Acts 17:28) is relational at every level, from the sub-atomic to the stars, from the intensely personal to the global movement of the world's economy. Indeed, the relational nature of reality and of every aspect of our existence is the reason Jesus' *way* has the power to transform our preoccupied, too often anxious, not quite fulfilled lives into something luminous.

> *I came that they may have life,*
> *and have it abundantly.*

> ⌁ John 10:10

I grew up going to church. I suppose that there has never been a time in my life when I was not a member of some church. But can I truly be a "Christian" if I do not believe in the factual truth of the statements made in the creeds and other traditional statements of belief? There are many who would say that I cannot. But if being a Christian means to live Christ's way, then, for the reasons to be explained, they are mistaken.

❧ 2 ❧

Are There Required Christian Beliefs?

It is commonly, and mistakenly, assumed that Christianity consists of a uniform set of fundamental beliefs. Although many assert that a person is a Christian only if he or she believes certain propositions, the particular propositions that one "must" believe have changed over the centuries and continue to change today. Christians—and there are two billion of them today—have always believed many different and often contradictory things.

Some Christians insist that the belief that Jesus was born of a virgin is absolutely essential to being a Christian, while others consider that belief irrelevant and misguided. Some Christians assert that one cannot be saved without being baptized, others do not. There are conflicts over the meaning of the Trinity, the authority of the church, whether there is a heaven or a hell, whether there is an afterlife. There are great differences over the meaning of "accepting Jesus" and "being saved." The Book of Acts and the letters of Paul, Peter, John, and Jude chronicled differences among the earliest followers of Jesus. The two-thousand-year history of Christianity is replete with disputes over beliefs.

There have been many efforts to establish agreement among Christians concerning beliefs. It seems that we humans have a strong urge to seek uniformity of belief. Perhaps it is because we feel more secure when others believe as we do, and we are troubled by those who challenge our beliefs. The need for other people to believe as one believes, and the fear of those whose beliefs differ, are powerful impulses. They have led to the redrawing of boundaries of communities and nations, to murder, and to religious wars.

Imposing uniformity of belief is a proven method of obtaining and maintaining political control. Three centuries after the death of Jesus, the emperor Constantine realized that controversies over belief threatened political stability in the Roman Empire. The most widespread disagreement in his time was between Christian followers of Arius, who believed Jesus was not divine, and followers of Athanasius, who asserted that Jesus had identity of being with God. To end this conflict Constantine called three hundred bishops to a meeting in Nicaea and demanded they agree on a uniform statement of what Christians should believe.

Constantine was not a theologian. His objective was not to impose a preselected set of his own beliefs. He wanted to obtain agreement because eliminating conflict between Christian factions would strengthen him politically. That meeting in 325 CE produced the Nicene Creed.

There have been, and are today, many creeds and statements of "correct" belief. To name only a few of them: the Apostles' Creed; the Athanasian Creed; the Augsburg Confession; the Scots Confession; the Heidelberg Catechism; Keach's Catechism; the Mennonite Confession of Faith; and the Anglican Thirty-Nine Articles of Religion.

The most widely known creed is the Nicene. It begins with the words: "We believe." Over the centuries since that creed was written and today, especially today, untold numbers have concluded that they cannot be Christians because they do not believe the contents of that creed to be factually true.

The First Council of Nicaea intended to produce a document that would establish uniformity of belief once and for all, but homogeneity proved impossible. The version adopted in 325 was revised in 381 by a second ecumenical council, the First Council of Constantinople. The First Council of Ephesus in 431 reaffirmed the version of 325. Between 325 and 787 there were seven ecumenical councils called to resolve differences in theology. And, of course, there always have been and will continue to be a multitude of conflicting interpretations of the Nicene Creed.

Disputes over "correct" belief have repeatedly divided Christianity. In 1204, the Catholic Church separated into the Roman Catholic Church and the Eastern Orthodox Church. A few hundred years later Roman Catholicism was fractured by Protestantism. Differences among Protestants have spawned hundreds of denominations.

The version of the Nicene Creed that is presently in use by English-speaking congregations of the Roman Catholic Church, the Episcopal Church, and the Evangelical Lutheran Church reads:

> We believe in one God,
> the Father, the Almighty,
> maker of heaven and earth,
> of all that is, seen and unseen.
>
> We believe in one Lord, Jesus Christ,
> the only Son of God,
> eternally begotten of the Father,
> God from God, Light from Light,
> true God from true God,
> begotten, not made,
> of one Being with the Father.
> Through him all things were made.
> For us and for our salvation
> he came down from heaven:
> by the power of the Holy Spirit
> he became incarnate from the Virgin Mary,
> and was made man.
> For our sake he was crucified
>   under Pontius Pilate;
> he suffered death and was buried.
> On the third day he rose again

in accordance with the Scriptures;
he ascended into heaven
and is seated at the right hand of the Father.
He will come again in glory to judge the living
        and the dead,
and his kingdom will have no end

We believe in the Holy Spirit, the Lord,
        the giver of Life,
who proceeds from the Father and the Son.
With the Father and the Son he is worshiped
        and glorified.
He has spoken through the Prophets.
We believe in one holy catholic and
        apostolic Church.
We acknowledge one baptism for the
        forgiveness of sins.
We look for the resurrection of the dead,
and the life of the world to come.

I have trouble with the creed as a factual statement, and I am not alone. A number of Christian denominations have dropped it from worship services. I once asked an adult discussion group at my church to review the creed line by line, noting what they accepted as true and what they did not. One person reported that he had "no problem" with every statement, but he did not wish to explain what he meant. Everyone else in this group of twenty committed church members found statements in the creed that they did not believe to be factually true.

Members of the group had many varying reservations and objections. Some objected to describing God as "father" because it was anthropomorphic, others on the ground that it is sexist, others because God is a mystery. Others disagreed with the statement that Jesus was the "only" Son of God because we are all children of God. Others did not think baptism was necessary to forgive sins. Still others objected to the assertion of virgin birth. Some pointed out that there had been an effort in the early writings to make Jesus' story match the Hebrew scriptures' prediction, in Isaiah, that a messiah would be born to a virgin, and that in Hebrew the same word is used to mean a young woman and a virgin. Others noted that requiring allegiance to an "apostolic" church, that is, a church led by bishops who selected their own successors, was a religious manifestation of a method of political control. Still others did not believe in the resurrection of the dead.

An ordained minister in the group said: "There is only one factual statement in the creed: 'He was crucified under Pontius Pilate; he suffered death and was buried,' but the rest is true even if it didn't happen." That postscript was consistent with the most common reaction of the members of the group, which was to say that the creed is metaphorically or poetically true.

Many who do not believe in the official creeds and catechisms think that it must follow that they cannot participate in the life of a Christian church community because it would be hypocritical to do so. But within Christianity there are scores of diverse beliefs, and to talk about divisions between recognized groups barely scratches the surface. In every congregation there are now and always have been individuals holding divergent beliefs. Within each individual Christian, at various times during a lifetime, beliefs vary. I doubt there is anyone who has precisely the same beliefs as an adult he or she did as a child.

Revering the Bible appears to be common to all Christians, but there is little agreement on its correct translation (there are many) or on its proper interpretation. Today those who believe that all the stories in the Bible are factually true constitute only a tiny minority of those who call themselves Christians. Yet millions reject Christianity because they incorrectly assume it requires accepting the stories in the Bible as literal truth.

There are other reasons for negative responses to Christianity. It is commonly assumed that being a Christian requires belief in a God who is essentially a superhuman being and who looks like the famous painting of the bearded God on the ceiling of the Sistine Chapel. Many do not accept that image. The existence of evil poses great difficulty for those who assume that to be a Christian you must believe in a God who is both loving and omnipotent. They reason that since a loving and omnipotent God would not allow evil to exist, they conclude that God does not exist.

Common to these doubts and outright rejections are unexamined and unsupported assumptions. All of us, whether believers, agnostics, or atheists, succumb to the error of assuming that God must have the characteristics we have imagined. When we do so we forget that we have only imposed our own ideas on God. We put too much faith in our own limited perceptions and reasoning. We assume that we, even though finite, limited beings, have the capacity to understand the nature of the infinite mystery in which we exist. As the Book of Job teaches, our ideas about God are, and can only be, inadequate.

Still another difficulty is that Christian institutions have been vehicles used to manipulate, to control, and to amass wealth and political power. Various understandings of Christianity have been used to justify intolerance in all its forms: slavery, discrimination, torture, and murder.

Yet despite these serious objections and concerns, people from every economic condition, from every level of intelligence, and from many varied cultures, have found something of enormous worth in Christianity. Many have found a "pearl of great price" (Matthew 13:45). Although the beliefs of Christians vary, it is indisputable that millions have been moved by Jesus' teachings. The survival of Christianity for twenty centuries leads to the conclusion that within the many conflicting interpretations of Christianity there is something important. Given the failure of Christians to agree on what to believe, it becomes necessary to look beyond creeds and catechisms for that pearl beyond price.

The Christian church (and in that term I include the many denominations) has historically focused on propositional belief, that is, on belief in statements such as: "Jesus was resurrected from the dead, ascended into heaven, sits on the right hand of God, and judges the living and the dead." But if we review Jesus' teachings and the ancient scriptures he quoted, we discover that his focus was not on propositional belief, but on the nature of our relationships with one another. The Christianity that emerges from what Jesus said and did is far removed from the Christianity often promulgated by public figures, both political and religious. Jesus' teachings are rightly viewed as the foundation of Christianity, but he made no attempt to reduce his *way* to a written statement of required factual beliefs. He was a student of scripture, but the parts of scripture that were important to him were not the stories of Moses' parting of the Red Sea, Jacob's ladder to heaven, the account of creation in seven days, Joshua's making the sun stand still, or Ezekiel's bringing dry bones back to life. He mentioned none of this. Jesus did not claim to have been born of a virgin or to have walked on water. Those were stories written many years after his death.

Jesus of Nazareth was concerned with bringing to life the deeper power of the scriptures we now call the Old Testament. And he was intent on doing so in this life, in the present, today.

> *So do not worry about tomorrow,*
> *for tomorrow will bring worries of its own.*
> ∼ Matthew 6:34

Jesus taught and exemplified a distinctive way of being in and relating to this world and through it he offered a means of experiencing this life in its most abundant dimension. The early Christians did not call themselves Christians. They called themselves "people of the way."

～ 3 ～

Truth

We usually associate "truth" with words, with statements, with propositions that we judge to be correct. This is the kind of truth I deal with as a lawyer. But the truth Jesus spoke of was of a different order. It was the truth of adopting a certain attitude, a particular perspective, the truth of doing, of practice. His truth was and is a truth to be lived, to be experienced.

When we love others,
we know that we belong to the truth.

～ 1 John 3:19 CEV

The one who believes in me
will also do the works that I do.

～ John 14:12

Everyone then who hears these words of mine and
acts on them will be like a wise man who built his
house on rock.

～ Matthew 7:24

The preeminent and indispensable "truth" that Jesus taught was to live life in loving relationship.

> One of them, a lawyer, asked him a question to test him. "Teacher, which commandment in the law is the greatest?" He said to him, "'You shall love the Lord your God with all your heart, and with all your soul, and with all your mind.' This is the greatest and first commandment. And a second is like it: 'You shall love your neighbor as yourself.' On these two command-ments hang all the law and the prophets."
>
> ∼ Matthew 22:35–40

In light of centuries of persecution of Jews by Christians, we need to pause to note that these statements, which are the heart, the *sine qua non,* of Jesus' ministry, are the teachings of classic Judaism. Jesus taught from Jewish scriptures that predated him by centuries. For the first commandment he cited Deuteronomy 6:4–5, known as the Shema, said by Jews for generations and still said today:

> Hear, O Israel: The LORD is our God, the LORD alone. You shall love the LORD your God with all your heart, and with all your soul, and with all your might.

For the second commandment he cited Leviticus 19:18:

> You shall not take vengeance or bear a grudge against any of your people, but you shall love your neighbor as yourself.

The common element that Jesus perceived in these two commandments was the adoption of a particular interior attitude: an attitude of loving-kindness.

Loving is not a belief. One can love without believing that Jesus walked on water or that Moses parted it. Loving is an outlook, an approach, a manner, a stance, a feeling, an attitude toward other people and the world we live in.

We shape and color everything we experience by our attitudes. We do not simply see another person or an object. We see a person we love, or hate, or fear, or like, or dislike, or are indifferent to. We see an object that, to our eyes, is beautiful or not, useful or not. Our internal state filters and affects every aspect of existence.

There is immense power in love because loving changes the lens through which we experience the world, and when we change that lens we change our world. Loving is a unique, and often difficult, way to relate to the world. Love is not about what statement or theology is "correct," but about relating to the world in a radically different way.

Belief is about knowledge. But love is not.

I pray that you may have the power to comprehend, with all the saints, what is the breadth and length and height and depth, and to know the love of Christ that surpasses knowledge, so that you may be filled with all the fullness of God.

~ Ephesians 3:18–19

Although the first commandment quoted by Jesus was "You shall love the Lord your God," Jesus did not fall into the trap of philosophizing about the nature of God. As a student of scripture he knew it was futile to try to reduce God to words or human understanding.

> *To whom then will you liken God, or what likeness compare with him?*
>
> ~ Isaiah 40:18

Job demanded an explanation, but did not get one.

> *Then the LORD answered Job out of the whirlwind: "Who is this that darkens counsel by words without knowledge?"*
>
> ~ Job 38:1–2

God would not give Moses his name, but replied: "I am who I am" (Exodus 3:14). God told Moses: "You cannot see my face; for no one shall see me and live" (Exodus 33:20).

Instead of being ensnared by the fruitless quest to reduce God to human images, ideas, and words, Jesus' focus throughout his ministry was on maintaining the interior attitude epitomized by love of neighbor.

But who is my neighbor?

Jesus was asked that question as soon as the words "love your neighbor" were out of his mouth. He answered this question in a way that demonstrates beyond argument that mere belief in religious precepts, in mere theology, in religious dogmas, however revered, must be subordinate to compassion. He answered with the famous story of the Good Samaritan (Luke 10:30–37).

The critical feature of that story is the contrast drawn between the actions of a Samaritan, who stopped to help the wounded man who had been attacked by thieves, and those of a priest and a Levite who passed by on the other side of the road. To fully appreciate the significance of this story we must understand that, in Jesus' community, the priest and Levite were revered as persons of correct religious belief and Samaritans were reviled as heretics, having broken from traditional Jewry in the sixth century BCE and constructed a separate temple on Mount Gerizim in Samaria. They had remained in Palestine when the mainstream Jews were deported for the Babylonian captivity. They rejected all the books of Jewish scripture after the Torah, the first five books of the Bible. At the time Jesus spoke there were hundreds of thousands of Samaritans in the Roman Empire, and they were at theological loggerheads with the Jews. Mainstream Jews considered their religious practices to be profane, a bastardization of Judaism. They did not observe Purim or Hanukkah. They married non-Jews.

By contrasting the Samaritan's compassionate conduct with that of the theologically correct priest and Levite, Jesus made it absolutely clear that it was the Samaritan's compassion, his caring relationship, that was decisive. "Correct" belief was irrelevant. It was even a hindrance to entering what Jesus called the kingdom of God within us, since, despite their lack of compassion, the priest and

Levite no doubt felt they were righteous because their beliefs were certifiably correct.

Jesus' consistent message throughout his ministry was that experience of the quality of life he called the "kingdom of God" is accessible not by dogma or correct belief, but only by the way of love of neighbor. He repeatedly ignored the religious strictures of his time in favor of the way of caring relationship. In violation of religious principles he healed on the Sabbath, he touched the leper, he spoke to the unaccompanied Samaritan woman at the well, he ate with the tax collector, he healed the Gentile Roman soldier's child, and he refused to condemn the woman caught in adultery. His rejection of propositional theology was entirely consistent with his way. He asked for something far different from, and far greater than, correct belief: he asked for the practice of love.

Jesus taught that if we could possess an interior attitude of love we would possess a treasure that could not be stolen or destroyed.

> *Do not store up for yourselves treasures on earth,*
> *where moth and rust consume and where thieves*
> *break in and steal; but store up for yourselves*
> *treasures in heaven, where neither moth nor rust*
> *consumes and where thieves do not break in and steal.*
> *For where your treasure is, there your heart will be*
> *also.*
>
> ~ Matthew 6:19–21

This "kingdom," this "treasure," this "pearl," is a way of being, a way of doing life. It is not to be found by espousing correct statements of belief; it can only be found by performing it. Jesus wrote nothing. He said:

I am the way, and the truth, and the life.

⁓ John 14:6

The author of the Gospel of John recognized this:

And the Word became flesh and lived among us.

⁓ John 1:14

As we have noted, loving is not a belief, it is a state of mind. Although love may be expressed in words, when the words "I love you" are sincere, they are the expression of an interior state. Their significance lies in the attitude that exists in the person saying them and in the consequences they cause in the hearer.

Love can turn our lives upside down. Think of the way your life was changed when you fell in love. In our experience of romantic love we have proof, in our own lives, of the power of love to change our way of being in the world.

This approach, this perspective, this *way* of relating to the world contains its own immense power. It not only changes the person, it can and has changed history—and it continues to do so. Mahatma Gandhi, a Hindu, reported in his autobiography that one of Leo Tolstoy's books, *The Kingdom of God Is Within You,* was one of the most important influences in his life. Approaching the British Raj without violence and with a call to its better self, Gandhi overturned the established order in India. Martin Luther King, Jr., a Christian minister, followed a similar path to awaken the conscience of America and break the back of institutional racism.

Through its power, love may reveal something that has been hidden or it may create that which did not exist before. The lover often sees something in the loved one that eludes everyone else. In a similar way, by caring we may see qualities in friends that others miss or ignore. Friendship, a form of loving-kindness, may bring out or create qualities that were not apparent or were nonexistent before.

Love remakes us and changes our experiences. Loving changes the caring person. The lover's point of view changes the object of care and the events of the day. It changes the experience of the loved one. Love is the essential and indispensible way to what Jesus called the "kingdom of God" because that kingdom is an internal state. We can only attain it by making this particular and exceptional inner change in ourselves.

There are, of course, degrees of love. Although I am incapable of achieving the degree of love exemplified by Jesus, I can try to move in that direction. I can offer kindness and good cheer to others. Despite my own failures, I can take "love" as a goal and count as movement toward that goal every act of consideration, however small. Although I cannot always, or even usually, maintain a truly loving attitude toward my neighbor, I can tell myself, with some expectation of at least partial success, to be kind, and to try to see things from the other person's point of view.

To "know" the other person is not to see them superficially, it is not to know some idea about them; it is to know them in their reality as living persons who transcend any label. We cannot know someone we understand only in terms of a label: fundamentalist, liberal, conservative, old, young, Hispanic, Jew, Christian, Muslim, Democrat, Republican, Catholic, Baptist, atheist, German, Russian, white, black, rich, poor, Chinese, Japanese...the categories are endless. We cannot truly know another person we view as a member of a category. We can only know the other person if we open ourselves to his or her unique individuality.

Jesus said: "If you had known me, you would have known my Father also" (John 14:7). In a dialogue with the disciples he explained what he meant by "knowing me." It had nothing to do with knowing theology or propositional belief and everything to do with sympathetic relationship. The disciples asked: "Lord, when was it that we saw you hungry or thirsty or a stranger or naked or sick or in prison, and did not take care of you?"

> *And he replied, "Just as you did not do it to one of the least of these, you did not do it to me."*
> ∽ Matthew 25:44–45

And the reverse is also true; even when we *do* care for others, we do not always see that we are caring for the God who dwells in them:

*I was hungry and you gave me food, I was thirsty and
you gave me something to drink, I was a stranger and
you welcomed me, I was naked and you gave me
clothing, I was sick and you took care of me, I was in
prison and you visited me.*

~ Matthew 25:35–36

"Do not judge," Jesus told his disciples (Mathew 7:1).
We are told not to judge because to judge is to subordinate
other people to our ideas about who they are. It is to fail
to be open to their reality which transcends our conclusions about them.

*God shows no partiality, but in every nation anyone
who fears him and does what is right is acceptable to
him.*

~ Acts 10:34–35

*There is no Jew or Greek, there is no longer slave or
free, there is no longer male and female; for you are
all one in Christ Jesus.*

~ Galatians 3:28

*In my Father's house there are many dwelling places.
If it were not so, would I have told you that I go to
prepare a place for you?*

~ John 14:2

We are daily bombarded with criticism and condemnation of the "other." It is the regular fare of newspaper
columns, blogs on the Internet, and talking heads on tel-

evision. Politicians manipulate voters by concentrating on issues that create fear and anger at "other" groups. But to buy into this culture is to allow our lives to be poisoned.

To improve the character of our unrepeatable experience of this life we must try to know our neighbors as the complex beings they are, transcending any label or system of thought, whether religious or political or philosophic. To truly know others we cannot dismiss them simply because they are not members of our ethnicity, or our political party, or our religious group.

Concepts and labels about other people always reduce and diminish their reality to abstractions. Love does no such thing. When we love our neighbor we engage with the reality of our neighbor, a person who is other, who is outside and beyond ourselves. Jesus insisted that everyone is our neighbor. It follows that judgmental forms of Christianity, in which those who do not believe "correctly" are condemned, are disastrously at odds with his message.

But we have been told that Christianity is the only way. Didn't Jesus himself say that?

Jesus said, "I am the way, and the truth, and the life. No one comes to the Father except through me."
　　　　　　　　　　　　　　　　　　∼ John 14:6

This particular verse has been used to justify an arrogant, exclusivist Christianity. That, in turn, has led to Catholics burning Protestants at the stake and Protestants beheading Catholics as well as other Protestants who believed differently, to ethnic cleansing and pogroms, to genocide and the Holocaust. But when Jesus said "I am the way to the Father" he was not speaking of the *way* as being belief in the Nicene Creed. The *way* he spoke of was not a dogma, not a set of propositions one must believe. Jesus' *way* was the way of love of neighbor.

The kingdom of God of which he spoke is an inner condition. It is an attitude, an outlook, a mindset, a mood, a way of being in the world. And it is absolutely true that we only enter that kingdom when we maintain an interior state of love. When this is understood, it can be correctly said, as Jesus did, that no one comes to the kingdom except his way: the way of loving-kindness. This mode of approaching the world and relating to our fellow beings is totally foreign to exclusivist, judgmental Christianity. When it is understood that he was speaking of living in love, a manner of living that transforms us and our world, it can be affirmed that Jesus' way is, in fact, the only way. It is not only the only way; it is also the universal way, open to anyone, even those who have never heard of Jesus.

~ 4 ~

Humility and Knowledge

We live in an age which venerates science, and many think that science and Christianity oppose each other. Some think that science has made the ultimate nature of reality comprehensible. Some think that their religious dogma has made the nature of God comprehensible. Both views are based on hubris.

Jesus' way of relating to the world requires humility, not only the humility to deflate our self-centeredness, but the humility to accept the limitations of our comprehension. It requires an intellectual humility which is at odds with those religious leaders and scientists who claim knowledge of the inherently unknowable.

The last century and a half of scientific development, from Michael Faraday and James Maxwell through Heinrich Hertz to Albert Einstein and beyond, has taught us many things, including the fact that Isaac Newton's ideas of absolute time and absolute space were wrong. Yet despite the enormous advances of science, we still do not comprehend this inexplicable, strange, and wonderful reality we call the world. If science has taught us anything, it has shown us that the more we know the more puzzling reality becomes.

When a molecule is split into two atoms and the spin of one atom is measured, the spin of the other will always be opposite, no matter how far apart they are. Albert Einstein wrote about this inexplicable action at a distance in the *Physics Review* in 1935, later calling it "spooky action at a distance." The experiment has been repeated many times, always with the same result. Thousands of words have been written about it, but no one understands how or why.

We have discovered that the materials that make up the earth and which constitute our own bodies were created by exploding stars. How is it that we have come to be created from stardust?

> *Then the* LORD *God formed man from the dust of the ground, and breathed into his nostrils the breath of life; and the man became a living being.*
>
> ⌇ Genesis 2:7

We glibly assert that the universe "began" with the big bang billions of years ago, but what caused the big bang? To our minds an effect without a cause is inconceivable. In that simple mental exercise we demonstrate our own limitations and the inadequacy of the mind to know the very things we often claim to know.

To us it seems impossible that the universe has no spatial dimensions. We cannot conceive of such a cosmos. It is impossible to visualize our universe as having no outer limit and equally impossible to visualize our universe as one that ends at some outer point. Try to do so. If the universe ends, what is on the other side of its limit? Not even Einstein could conceive of a universe without limit, so he theorized space as curving back on itself.

For mortals it is impossible, but for God all things are possible.

∼ Matthew 19:26

What is impossible for human reason to comprehend is nonetheless possible. Our astronomers peer into their telescopes and see that the impossible, a universe without limit, simply is. In 1996 the Hubble Deep Space Team reported that a long-term photograph of an apparently empty area of the sky, an area the size of a dime viewed seventy-five feet away, revealed at least fifteen hundred galaxies. Their news release was careful to say "at least" because there were certainly galaxies existing beyond the limit of the telescope. And let's not pass quickly over the concept of a galaxy. Our own galaxy, the Milky Way, is apparently typical, and it contains four hundred billion stars and is one hundred thousand light years in diameter.

At the other end of the continuum we find that all the objects we deal with are made of molecules, molecules are made of atoms, atoms contain a nucleus made of protons and neutrons, and protons and neutrons are made of even smaller quantum objects that pop in and out of existence. Quantum objects may be perceived as either wave or particle, depending on the perspective of the observer.

And in the word "perceived" we arrive at another significant limitation in our understanding. We perceive, through our five senses, only a limited spectrum of wavelengths. Everything we deal with on a daily basis—the food we eat, the air we breathe, the water we drink, the people we meet—fall within that spectrum. But through devices such as radio telescopes we learn that there are many other wavelengths.

Science has taught us that, contrary to the assumptions of many thoughtful people a century ago, that which exists cannot be reduced to or explained by matter alone. Complex physical systems give rise to effects that cannot be explained in terms of their constituent parts. The properties of the human brain, such as consciousness, thought, rationality, and sensations, are of a different order than the nerve cells that make it up. Reduce any living creature, whether plants or human beings, to its parts and something that previously existed will disappear. Yet when it existed that "something" was just as real as its material parts. We can observe this, we can give it names, but we cannot recapture that which was once present.

Acknowledgment of our limitations destroys the barriers that our judgments and unfounded ideas have erected—the high, unseen walls that divide us based on differing beliefs. When we fully appreciate how little we know and how completely dependent we are on that which we do not comprehend, then, regardless of the words we might use to express belief or non-belief, we are religious in the sense that we rightly feel our "absolute dependence" on infinitude.[2]

Who has known the mind of the Lord?
                                        ∽ Romans 11:34

We do not know what we do not know. While this statement, at first glance, seems to repeat itself, it should expose our blindness to our own blindness. It reminds us of the lack of foundation for the materialism that dominates our thinking, that paradigm that prevents us from seeing the ineffable that begins "where the possible *for us* ends, where what human reason comprehends as *possible for it* comes to a halt, at the precise limit where our thought can no longer advance, or see, or speak—where the inaccessible domain of the impossible bursts open."[3]

~ 5 ~

The Limits of
Our Languages

When Pilate asked, "What is truth?" (John 18:38), Jesus remained silent. We live in a world dominated and constrained by languages. We use mathematical, scientific, and verbal languages to express our ideas about religion and about the world. Languages are necessary for the functioning of the economy, to link us to others, to earn our livings, to live in community, and for countless other purposes.

I once thought I would someday be able to answer the question: What is the meaning of life? Eventually I abandoned the search to answer this question because I realized I had no answer. But it haunted me. I thought that surely philosophers or theologians would have the answer. Later, many years later, I began to understand that the problem is that answering the question requires expression in language, and language, whether verbal, scientific, or mathematical, is not up to the task.

There are a number of levels of the inadequacy of language.

We often assume the meanings of the words we use are common, shared meanings. But words have variable meanings, and we construe them in many diverse ways. Suppose you and I were to discuss these well-known words of the English poet John Keats in his "Ode on a Grecian Urn":

Beauty is truth, truth beauty,—that is all
Ye know on earth, and all ye need to know.

What is truth? What is beauty? It is likely that we would find that these words have a different meaning to each of us.

There is an even greater chance for difference and variability if, instead of comparing our reading of a single phrase, we compared our interpretations of an essay or a poem or a novel. Think of how frequently such differences occur in high school and college literature classes.

And it is not just between persons that such differences may arise. Someone who is happy may read a particular text and take away one message, and the same person, reading during a time of stress, may take away another. In speaking about the experience of reading scripture, the French philosopher Emmanuel Levinas wrote that words may contain "an inexhaustible surplus of meaning."[4]

The problem goes beyond varied meanings and interpretations. A central and serious problem is that we often assume that our languages are accurate depictions of reality. But in fact no language completely corresponds to the reality it attempts to depict. Words, equations, and scientific theories are abstractions, and thus reductions, diminutions, of reality.

We are caught in a spider's web of languages, of connected symbols. This is true of all our languages, whether religious, cultural, scientific, or professional. And we frequently forget that our words are inadequate representations of reality.

The word "tree" is not the same as the oak outside my window. No matter how careful I am in my description, no number of words, even brilliantly chosen words, can perfectly represent the tree. There are multiple levels to consider: the tree itself, my mental image of it, my description of it, and your mental image of the oak tree. None correspond exactly to the other. The problem is further compounded when I speak to you about your image of that tree. It may have many features in common with mine, but it will never be the same. Neither of us can capture the complete reality of the tree.

As Flaubert wrote in *Madame Bovary,*

> Language is like a cracked kettle on which we beat
> out tunes for bears to dance to, while all the time
> we long to move the stars to pity.

Beliefs are expressed in language. Much of the history of religion in general and of Christianity in particular is a history of controversy over words. For centuries Catholics and Protestants have been disagreeing with each other and among themselves over the "correct" statements of belief and interpretations of scripture. Quarreling over words dates to the very beginning of this movement we call Christianity.

> *Whoever teaches otherwise and does not agree with the sound words of our Lord Jesus Christ and the teaching that is in accordance with godliness, is conceited, understanding nothing, and has a morbid craving for controversy and for disputes about words.*
>> ∼ 1 Timothy 6:3–4

Words, no matter how brilliant or how sacred, are abstractions, and reality is ultimately beyond our descriptions and thoughts. Although I may use the same words to talk about God as those used by my next-door neighbor, or my brother, or my wife, our images and ideas will differ, and none of them will correspond to the reality of the ultimate mystery we so blithely name "God."

> *Anyone who claims to know something does not yet have the necessary knowledge.*
>> ∼ 1 Corinthians 8:2

You and I may be members of the same church, we may share the same pew, we may say the same words, we may be looking at the same images in the same stained glass windows. Your interpretation of those words and images, and the ideas they trigger in you, may be similar to mine, but they will never be the same. As members of a given church we may think we are worshiping the same

God, but the images and ideas of God held by each of us will never be precisely the same.

There have been many attempts to speak about the nature of God. Here are a few from noted philosophers and theologians (with apologies to them for oversimplifying):

For Charles Hartshorne, the word "God" refers to a series of events in which God becomes the world.

For Richard Kearney, the word "God" refers to that which makes possible, enables, empowers.

For Bernard Loomer, the word "God" refers to the ultimate mystery inherent within existence itself.

For Paul Tillich, the word "God" refers to the "ground of being."

For Alfred North Whitehead, the word "God" refers to the empowering and saving event in which the universe creatively constitutes itself.

For John Cobb, the word "God" refers to the nexus of events, a living happening, providing the possibility for adventure in the world.

For Marjorie Suchocki, the word "God" refers to the influence of the creative and redemptive future.

For Henry Nelson Wieman, the word "God" refers to the occurrence of creative transformation, the creative good, through which good can emerge within the world.

For Sallie McFague, the word "God" refers to the spirit that moves in all things.

For Dietrich Bonhoeffer, the word "God" refers to the beyond in the midst of life.

When Einstein was asked about religion, he said: "To know that what is impenetrable to us really exists, manifesting itself as the highest wisdom and the most radiant beauty, which our dull facilities can comprehend only in the most primitive forms—this knowledge, this feeling, is at the center of true religiousness. In this sense, and in this sense only, I belong in the ranks of devoutly religious men."[5]

Certain contemporary physicists have suggested, in a good faith attempt to speak of the ultimate, that it is the "zero-point field." By this they refer to a field deduced from the Heisenberg uncertainty principle. Pursuant to that principle everything that is, is ultimately an assembly, not of atoms, but something even more ephemeral— quantum "objects." Because of quantum fluctuations, every quantum object always has some energy. Even in outer space there is no true vacuum; always and everywhere this residual electromagnetic energy pops in and out of existence. These ceaseless electromagnetic waves represent a far greater amount of energy than that contained in all the galaxies and it is their presence that is referred to as the "zero-point field." This field is seen by these scientists as both the original and continuing cause of material existence. But, as the physicist Niels Bohr put it:

> There is no quantum world. There is only an abstract physical description. It is wrong to think that the task of physics is to find out how nature is. Physics concerns what we can say about nature.[6]

Theologies and religions are made up of words, ideas, symbols, and images. And so also are sciences. No matter how holy or true we consider them, they are merely constructions of the human mind. Buried inside all our languages are unchallenged and unproven assumptions taken on faith. Even the most committed materialist is making a statement based on faith when asserting that nothing lies outside what we can perceive and understand.

When we reduce anything to formulas or equations, or a name, we often fool ourselves into thinking we comprehend whatever it is that we have spoken of. We have an almost overwhelming predisposition to do this. But complete understanding of reality can never occur. This is true about the oak tree in my yard. It is true of that complex person who is my neighbor. It is true of the mystery we call God.

Martin Heidegger, one of the seminal philosophers of the twentieth century, wrote that the erroneous assumption that we can discover ultimate, foundational truth lies at the very heart of Western philosophy. He called that error "ontotheology." Today none of our greatest thinkers assert that there is some system of thought that rests on an unshakable foundation. There is no such system. If there were, it would be widely known.

As recognized both by Eastern religious leaders and contemporary scientists, another captivating idea about the nature of the ultimate focuses on consciousness. We know that all we observe as the physical world is the product of our consciousness tuned to recognize a limited spectrum of the many frequencies that exist. When we see, hear, touch, taste, and smell, we use that which we call consciousness, and it somehow converts these frequencies into meaning. Meaning is expressed in language. Both consciousness and language present unanswered and unanswerable questions. We do not understand how consciousness evolved from primordial matter. We do not understand how it converts perceptions into language. If consciousness of an object renders it either a particle or a wave, did one or the other exist before perception?

We say that the universe consists of objects, quantum or otherwise, of fields, of wavelengths. By naming we convince ourselves we understand. But do we? We talk of time as if we understand time. Einstein discovered that time is relative to the gravitational pull of objects, so what does it mean to speak of "before" anything existed?

These and similar questions demonstrate our limitations. Even to declare these questions meaningless, out of bounds, is to reveal our limitations.

Science may appear to provide hard facts about the world, but scientific ideas are projections and abstractions.

So too are religious ideas. We imagine a variety of characteristics for God or the Ultimate or Reality, whether we call them matter and energy or consciousness, whether we name the infinite as Jesus or Spirit or Allah, whether we understand God as the "zero-point field" or the Old Man in the Sky. All these images tell us something about ourselves, but they do not tell us anything about God. This is not to make a point about God. It is to make a point about the limitations of our words, our ideas, our formulas, our images—ourselves.

In his popular book *A Brief History of Time,* the physicist Stephen Hawking assumed he knew what the word "God" refers to. But all he did was engage in circular reasoning. He decided that he knew what the term "God" refers to, and that it refers to a being that could not exist, thus he "concluded" that God does not exist.

Hawking was correct in one respect: the God he was thinking of does not exist. The God referred to in books by popular authors who debunk the so-called "God myth" also does not exist. The concept of God that is so often attacked is a cartoon character.

Claiming that any image or idea, much less one's religion or scientific theory, is the truth is a refusal to recognize our limits. It is to claim that we have the capacity to attain ultimate knowledge, and it is to claim that we can diminish reality to our abstractions, to our words, to our equations, to our ideas. But that claim is pure hubris—the deadliest of the seven deadly sins. To believe that one's images and ideas about God are an exposition of final truth is to sanctify and worship our own creations.

> *They exchanged the truth about God for a lie and*
> *worshiped and served the creature rather than the*
> *Creator, who is blessed forever!*
>
> ∼ Romans 1:25

Job, like us, wanted an explanation, but he did not get one.

> *"O that I had one to hear me!*
> *Let the Almighty answer me!"*
>
> ∼ Job 31:35

> *Then the Lord answered Job out of the whirlwind:*
> *"Who is this that darkens counsel by words without*
> *knowledge?"*
>
> ∼ Job 38:1–2

Any statement I make, any thought I have, about the ultimate nature of all reality must fall infinitely short of the mark. The first three commandments have been saying to us, for thousands of years:

> *I am the Lord your God, . . . you shall have no other*
> *gods before me. You shall not make for yourself an*
> *idol, whether in the form of anything that is in heaven*
> *above, or that is on the earth beneath, or that is in the*
> *water under the earth. You shall not bow down to*
> *them or worship them. . . . You shall not make*
> *wrongful use of the name of the Lord your God.*
>
> ∼ Exodus 20:2–7

We cannot avoid forming ideas and pictures in our minds about God or using language to talk about God. Likewise, we cannot avoid forming ideas and pictures in our minds about reality or using language to talk about reality. But when we take our ideas for *the* truth about reality we make them into something more than they are.

This habit has done unimaginable harm. Throughout history religious figures claiming to possess *the* truth have justified murder and warfare. Even today religious fanatics commit acts of terrorism in the name of their beliefs. It is not just in the religious sphere that assuming one possesses *the* truth causes harm. Accepting materialism as final and definitive makes it appear that we live in a desolate, meaningless world, and thus diminishes our experience of each irreplaceable and miraculous day.

The ideas many of our contemporaries have about God have caused them to abandon Christianity. As noted earlier, the traditional Christian ideas of God require God to be both loving and omnipotent. Many people believe that surely such a God would not allow evil. Thus, since evil exists, it follows that God does not exist. This is the position of the contemporary author and New Testament scholar Bart D. Ehrman in his book *God's Problem: How the Bible Fails to Answer Our Most Important Question— Why We Suffer.*[7] But where did we get the notion that we have understanding sufficient to impose our ideas on God? God would not be God if God can be confined to our ideas and to that which we can comprehend.

In his *Confessions,* Saint Augustine asked, as we may: What do I love when I love my God? But he had no answer. Clear-eyed evaluation of our circumstances reveals that we do not know anything in sufficient depth to claim ultimate comprehension. To the contrary, daily we accept the world, the universe, and all that life offers: on faith.

We do not wait to comprehend before we live. First we live. As the philosopher John Caputo has observed: "Life is carried along by the impulse of faith, by the passion of faith, and we will not take a single step forward, *le pas au-delà,* without faith."[8] The reference to *le pas au-delà* (the step not beyond) is to the title of a book by Maurice Blanchot, a French philosopher who wrote of the paradoxes of literature and language. Blanchot noted that our vision of reality is warped by words because, through words, we make reality abstract.

Our existence is a gift. The world is a gift. We accept these gifts every time we draw a breath. We take these gifts on a trust that precedes and transcends understanding. The desire to understand, to know, to investigate the source of these gifts comes later, if at all. The world around us, even the seemingly mundane, especially the mundane, is primary, and we take it on faith. Do we stop to understand how our food and drink came to be and how and why it is provided to us, before we trust our lives to it?

All systems of thought, whether philosophy, religion, science, or mathematics, are based on axioms, hypotheses, and assumptions that cannot be proven, that are taken on faith. This has been demonstrated to be true even in mathematics and geometry. In 1931, the mathematician Kurt Gödel published his two famous incompleteness theorems, stating that any self-consistent system such as mathematics or geometry will contain true propositions that cannot be proven from the system's axioms. Gödel expressed it simply: "There are some truths that cannot be proven to be true."

In his famous *Tractatus Logico-Philosophicus*, Ludwig Wittgenstein concluded that language can only reflect the world, thus any attempt to use words to describe what lies outside the world is impossible. Trying to explain language with language is also impossible for the same reason. The *Tractatus* concludes: "What we cannot speak about we must pass over in silence."[9]

In his later book *Philosophical Investigations,* said by many to be the most important philosophical work of our time, Wittgenstein showed how we are imprisoned by our own words, by our languages.[10] This is true whether we refer to the languages of philosophy, science, religion, business, politics, or any of our other communal systems of words. Our paradigms may shift from time to time, but we cannot escape being enmeshed in our systems of language. We cannot transcend them to some higher, outside, foundational place.

This has been recognized since the Greek mathematician and philosopher Archimedes made this point by asserting that he could lift the world *if* he were given a solid place to stand and a long lever. Of course there is no such place. There simply is no vantage point "outside" us from which the whole can be seen. As René Descartes pointed out in his *Second Meditation* and, as countless others have known, we can never separate ourselves from our context and concepts to arrive at an Archimedean point beyond ourselves that would allow us to comprehend the whole and thus determine the ultimate truth of our ideas.

The failure to recognize this is to massively and disastrously overvalue human capability. It is to presume that we have the ability to acquire ultimate understanding, to truly have knowledge of ultimate reality and its ultimate meaning. It is to act as if, because we have eaten of the tree of knowledge, we are God's equal.

Languages of every sort often evoke mental images. The language used by Christianity evokes an image of God in human terms, as Jesus or a beneficent Old Man in the Sky. But from a biblical perspective we are not required to accept the image of God as a being with a human face, or even as a "being," that is, as something or someone that we comprehend; to the contrary, the Bible repeatedly warns against certainty about images and knowledge of God:

> *To whom then will you liken God, or what likeness compare with him?*
>
> ~ Isaiah 40:18

> *Where is the one who is wise? Where is the scribe? Where is the debater of this age? Has not God made foolish the wisdom of the world? For since, in the*

wisdom of God, the world did not know God through
wisdom.

                             ~ 1 Corinthians 1:20–22

We know that "all of us possess knowledge."
Knowledge puffs up, but love builds up. Anyone who
claims to know something does not yet have the
necessary knowledge.

                             ~ 1 Corinthians 8:1–2

The Bible repeatedly condemns our propensity to over-value our ability to know. The stories of Adam and Eve's fall, of the Tower of Babel, of the failures of Job's comforters, and of God's refusal to allow Moses to see him or to know his name all have this common theme, as do the repeated admonitions in the psalms and the explicit orders of the first three commandments.

How unsearchable are God's judgments and how
inscrutable his ways!

                             ~ Romans 11:33

Nevertheless, throughout history there have been many who have made the mistake of believing that their group has attained *the* truth. Tragically, there have also been too many who have made the terribly dangerous error of believing that it is their duty to impose their beliefs on others, or worse, to destroy those who believe differently. Today we see this in the actions of Muslim extremists, but the disease has long infected Christianity, too. In the past it motivated the Crusades and the Inquisition, while in the present it appears whenever someone claims that it is God's will that homosexuals die of AIDS, or insists that non-believers are bound for the flames of hell. Fundamentalism of this sort is heretical in the extreme because it is based on accepting human ideas and images as divine. It is idolatry.

Atheists commit a similar error. Like their fundamentalist counterparts, atheists assume that the human mind is able to answer to the ultimate questions, particularly the question of God, and they too are guilty of hubris. They believe that they have the answer, which is that there is nothing other than the world as they understand it.

Agnostics make a slightly different error when they say they are ready to have faith in God, but only if a proof of God, an intelligible exposition of the ultimate, is provided to them. Yet in this "if" they have assumed that the human mind is capable not only of understanding ultimate truth, but also of articulating it.

For these reasons the God I am speaking of here is the God we see in the book of Exodus, the God who is beyond our thoughts, words, images, and ideas. It is the God whose name is so holy that the Jewish members of our shared religion understood that it could not be written or spoken, the God for whom they devised the unpronounceable symbol Y*H*V*H.

Does God exist? To pose the question is to assume that God can be captured in our words, in our thoughts. As the Catholic priest, theologian, and philosopher Raimundo Panikkar noted: "To speak of God, even for the purpose of denying God's existence, is to 'transform' God into the order of creatures, and so is tantamount to destroying God."[11]

Acceptance of the limits of human understanding should restore our rightful state: a state of humility in the face of a reality so deeply enigmatic, so fantastic, and so incomprehensibly strange, so *wonder* filled, that no text, no creed, no equation, no formula, no scientific concept, no philosophy, and no theology can encompass it. As Saint Anselm put it in his *Proslogion*:

> Lord, you are not merely that
> than which a greater cannot be thought;
> you are something greater than can be thought.

～ 6 ～

Presence

The eternal mystery is always present. It is only hidden from us because we are usually sleepwalking. It is continuous and all encompassing. It is as close as our own bodies. Neuroscience tells us that the eyes do not transmit a picture to the brain. The eyes are merely light receptors; it is the brain that "sees." The astronomer Carl Sagan was fond of pointing out that the materials that make us up originated from cosmic explosions. But how and why did stardust become brain cells, and how did those cells learn to take light impulses and organize them? What is "in" the material of those cells that gives them the ability to imbue the data with meaning? How does that happen as I read or as I write?

How did some cells know to become nerves, and others bone, cornea, muscle, skin, liver, heart, hair, colon, or fingernails? How do the organs in our bodies know to function together to extract energy from food? How do some cells know to become an amoeba? How does an amoeba know to trap and destroy an infectious bacterium? How did those abilities evolve from the dust of stars?

I take a breath. As the atoms in a molecule of oxygen cross the cell barrier in my lungs, they instantly become a part of me, a living creature. I exhale. Those atoms are expelled. How is it that they are no longer alive?

What am I? Not a single cell that constituted my body over seven years ago is still a part of me. My feelings and thoughts change frequently. My personality may, in many respects, be similar to that of the child I once was, but it is not the same.

Philosophers such as Alfred North Whitehead in modern times, and Heraclitus in ancient Greece, would say that I am a "process," but does describing me with this word, or any word, mean that I am understood? We think we understand evolution because we say it is a process, but do we know what is inherent in lifeless stardust that caused that amazing process to unfold over billions of years?

Something we call "gravity" holds my body to the surface of the earth, holds the earth in orbit around the sun, and acting over unimaginable distances of thousands of light years, holds the sun in orbit around the center of the Milky Way galaxy. We see its effects, we have a name for it, but no one knows how it extends its invisible power over inconceivable distances.

What we think of as empty space is actually teeming with energy. Every part of it is filled with light visible to the naked eye. We can verify that by recalling that we can see the lights of the same stars, millions of them, regardless of where we happen to be as we ride the earth in its annual orbit around the sun.

Each cubic inch of the universe, including our own bodies, is filled with wavelengths, most of which are detectable only with instruments. The physicist David Bohm noted: "If one computes the amount of energy that would be in one cubic centimetre of space, with this shortest possible wavelength, it turns out to be very far beyond the total energy of all the matter in the known universe."[12] But no one knows how or why.

We can see the effects of the creative unknown at every level, from our fingernails to clusters of galaxies, but we do not know how or why rudimentary material elements organize into more complex systems.

At any moment of our lives, wherever we are, we can awake and realize that we live in a world that exceeds all our theologies and sciences. This is not a new insight. For thousands of years the Bible has insisted that we become conscious of this truth.

An Indian myth is that the world rests on the back of a giant tiger, and the tiger stands on the back of a giant turtle. The story is told that when the oldest and wisest guru was asked by a child, "What supports the turtle?" the guru answered, "It's turtles all the way down." Of course it is. And it might also be quantum particles all the way "down" or "up." Only through our minds' images can we speak of the incomprehensible.

The depth of the great unknown, that cannot be named, which some of us call God, does not prevent us from experiencing its presence. Whatever my image and thoughts may be of God, or of Y*H*V*H, of ultimate reality, or of nature, by whatever name I might use, this enigma in which "we live and move and have our being" (Acts 17:28) is here, now, surrounding me and constituting all that I am and all that is.

We all have images and ideas about the ultimate nature of the world, and they profoundly affect us. What words do we use when we think about the cause of all that is? Do we speak of God, or Nature, or Evolution, or Spirit, or Reality, or Mystery, or something else? Does our image suggest that existence is meaningless or purposeful, uncaring or beneficent? Whatever it is, it is merely our own imperfect creation, formed from the raw materials of our experiences and our culture.

We cannot think without images. For some of us these continue to be the traditional religious images. They were accepted by my parents. Can we appreciate our limitations and still form an image of God that comforts us? Can we talk to that God? How much richer would our lives be if we had the kind of relationship with God in which we could speak to the one we imagine? It is hardly surprising that the image of God as a person has such a hold on the mind. There is no reason why we should not speak to our image of God, whatever it may be. Even if the traditional image is one we reject, the Mystery in which we live and move has provided us with words and the ability to speak them.

For me, thinking of the presence of the surrounding Mystery brings comfort. The poet Denise Levertov must have found reassurance there too. In her poem "Primary Wonder" she said it this way:

Days pass when I forget the mystery.
Problems insoluble and problems offering
their own ignored solutions
jostle for my attention, they crowd
        its antechamber
along with a host of diversions, my
        courtiers, wearing
their colored clothes; caps and bells.
                        And then
once more the quiet mystery
is present to me, the throng's clamor
recedes: the mystery
that there is anything, anything at all,
let alone cosmos, joy, memory, everything,
rather than void: and that, O Lord,
Creator, Hallowed One, You still,
hour by hour sustain it.[13]

∼ 7 ∼

In What Can
I Believe?

If all our religious and scientific ideas are inadequate, if all our knowledge is inherently partial, if there is no answer to so many important questions, isn't there something we can distill into words and say: "In this I believe"?

But is religious belief necessary? To form the question more precisely, is it necessary that we have religious beliefs that can be put into words?

If we cannot articulate our beliefs in words, are we left in a valueless condition? As we have seen, even science is based on unproven assumptions. We seem to be presented with a Hobson's choice: either we commit ourselves to some unverifiable system of belief, or we accept complete relativism, in which no absolute truth is even possible. As a result of our need for certainty and security, isn't it inevitable that we choose religious beliefs of some kind? And if so, which system of belief should we choose?

There are many belief systems, both secular and religious, and an exploration of the most common systems is only the beginning. Whether the prescribed systems are expressed in creeds, catechisms, and holy texts or in equations, formulas, and scientific texts, each is an abstraction reflecting only a part of this multifaceted and puzzling world. To avoid complexity, some groups attempt to encapsulate their belief systems in an apparently straightforward command such as: "Believe in Jesus, so that you can be saved" or "Accept Jesus as your personal savior." But when examined carefully such statements mean different things to different people. Even within the most stringently policed religious groups, a close examination will show that beliefs vary somewhat from minister to minister, priest to priest, rabbi to rabbi, imam to imam.

Nevertheless, in the religious sphere many of us have a great need to be able to say: "This is what I believe." Institutional Christianity has offered to fill that need with creeds, catechisms, and articles of faith. In my church we say the Nicene Creed, and it provides us with three ways of imagining God: God as Father, God as Son, and God as Holy Spirit. But if we cannot capture a tree, or our neighbor, or the endless universe with words and ideas, we surely cannot capture God.

Faith, whether religious or scientific, must not be the arrogant faith suggested by Job's comforters, or one thrust on us by those we often see on Sunday morning television. Our faith cannot claim, as they seem to, that we possess *the* truth, and we know God's will. That conceit has led to bigotry, intolerance, inquisitions, and religious wars.

> *Beware of false prophets. . . . You will know them by their fruits.*
>
> ⮬ Matthew 7:15–16

When we use human words, images, and ideas to refer to God or to the ultimate nature of the universe, and we cannot avoid this, we must humbly remind ourselves that "we see in a mirror, dimly" (1 Corinthians 13:12). We do the best we can because that is all we can do. To admit that we do not know is not to abandon the search for greater truth or to deny that truth exists. It is to recognize that as finite, contextual beings, none of us will ever possess complete truth. Generally, the way we judge whether something is true is by determining if it is consistent with our experience and knowledge. And, of course, our experience and understanding is always evolving and always relative to, and limited by, the information we have, our education, culture, history, and language. The best any of us can ever do is to begin from where we are, and act and think in the context of our circumstances and experiences.

This is an age-old point. Recall the ancient story of the blind men describing the elephant. The one who held its trunk said it felt like a snake. The one who touched its side said it felt like a wall. The one who held its leg said it felt like a tree. All were partially correct, but each was wrong in believing that he had described the whole animal. In 1872 John Godfrey Saxe wrote a famous version of the poem called "The Blind Men and the Elephant," which concludes: "So oft in theologic wars, / The disputants, I ween, / Rail on in utter ignorance / Of what each other mean, / And prate about an Elephant / Not one of them has seen."

We often fail to recognize the relative and limited nature of human understanding. This is true not only when thinking about religion, whether pro or con, but also in thinking about science. Today we tend to associate science with proven facts and unassailable conclusions about what is true, but do we give current theories too much credence? The track record of science is not reassuring.

Many scientists are convinced that they have the intellectual tools to discover all there is to know. They have thought that in the past, too. Theory after theory about the nature of the world has been proven wrong: It was once "common knowledge" that the earth is flat, that the earth is the center of the universe, that matter is made up of smaller bits of matter, that time is absolute, that time is eternal, that mass and energy are not equivalent, that the universe is in a steady state, that the temperature of outer space is absolute zero.

In our own everyday lives, we regularly accept our culture's common ideas and images as the truth. The predominant philosophy underlying our culture's current ideas and images is materialism. Materialism is more than valuing, or overvaluing, money and material goods. It is a philosophy based on the belief that there is nothing beyond the material world, and all that is can be explained in terms of matter. Both materialism and dogmatic religions assume that their representations of the world, their belief systems, are *the* truth, failing to recognize that their beliefs, whether expressed in creeds or in equations, are simply models or maps of the world, not the world itself.

We all have many beliefs. We cannot function without them. Do we believe that food will be available at our local grocery tomorrow? That our family will support us emotionally? Financially? That our homes will continue to have electricity? That Frank is a crook, that Henry can be trusted? Do we believe that life is meaningful or meaningless? Our beliefs are the basis for every decision, every relationship, every action we take.

Because our systems of belief are so deeply embedded in all we do and all we are, we are usually unconscious of them. However, there have always been some among us, even among religious leaders, who understand the limitations of human ideation. A recent example is found in a 2006 pastoral letter from Bishop Frank Griswold, then Presiding Bishop of the Episcopal Church of the United States, to those Episcopalians who were asserting that only their interpretation of scripture could possibly be correct. He wrote: "It is important for Episcopalians on all sides to realize that truth in its fullness cannot be contained in any one perspective."

The traditional Christian denominations in the United States and Europe have been losing members for decades. Great numbers of one-time church members have left because they think that to participate without hypocrisy it is necessary to believe that the biblical accounts and the traditional creeds are factually true. While this may be true of some Christian organizations, there are many Christian communities that do not read the Bible and the creeds as factual statements. Their refusal to do so is the result of a wise understanding, sometimes conscious, sometimes intuitive, of the limits of doctrine, of words, and, ultimately, of the human mind.

Meaning is always expressed in language, but as we have seen, languages are mere pointers at reality, chimeras as variable and changeable as quicksilver. An approach to both theology and language that reflects this is illustrated by a decision made in 1559 by Queen Elizabeth I. Elizabeth, a Protestant, succeeded to the English throne following the reign of her half-sister, Mary Tudor, a Catholic. Mary Tudor is known as "Bloody Mary" because she attempted to enforce her brand of religion, which she believed was the one true religion, by means of persecution, torture, and murder.

Although Elizabeth was a Protestant and opposed to Catholic extremism, she also opposed Protestant extremism. As Queen of England she was both the head of state and head of the church, and she sought to bring a measure of peace and tolerance in her realm. In response to the ongoing conflict between Protestants and Catholics she famously said, "I have no desire to make windows into men's souls." Her solution to religious strife is known as the Elizabethan Settlement, whereby both Catholics and Protestants used the same churches and the same prayer book, but it was a revised prayer book. It had been reworded in such a way that disputed words in the liturgies could be interpreted to mean one thing by Catholics and another by Protestants.

The genius of the Elizabethan Settlement in 1559 was the recognition that any text may have multiple meanings, and each individual's perception of the meaning of a text depends upon the reader's perspective, as shaped by his or her background. Implicit in this approach was the idea that religious words are *legitimately* open to multiple understandings. And, most significantly for our purposes, at the heart of this approach was a determination that peaceful relationship with one's neighbor was more important than uniform belief.

The Elizabethan Settlement was both a religious and a political event. As a religious statement, it was grounded in biblical orthodoxy in which harmonious relationship trumps doctrinal statements of belief.

> *For the whole law is summed up in a single commandment: "You shall love your neighbor as yourself."*
>
> ~ Galatians 5:14

The Elizabethan Settlement was not the first time that the malleability of words had been used to reconcile conflicting beliefs. When Constantine called three hundred bishops to the Council at Nicaea in the year 325 his principal objective was to resolve the controversy between followers of Arius, who believed Jesus was not God, and followers of Athanasius, who asserted that Jesus had "identity of being" with God. The words ultimately selected for the Nicene Creed asserted that Jesus and God were "one in being." That phraseology could be read by each group to be consistent with its beliefs, and all but two of the three hundred bishops signed that creed.

We should not make the mistake of thinking that religious leaders in 325 and 1559 were somehow duped into accepting ambiguity through clever wording. Among their numbers were some of the most well-educated and thoughtful people of their times. They were sincere advocates of differing points of view. Yet they consciously and conscientiously sought concord.

The Elizabethan Settlement and the Council of Nicaea are but two examples of many that reflect an approach to theology that recognizes the limitations of our words and ideas, an approach that subordinates words and ideas to the basic human need and desire to live together in harmony. But it is an approach often criticized for its failure to provide definite, concrete answers. We crave certainty, but that craving makes us vulnerable to manipulation and control by those who claim to provide it.

But if all words can have multiple meanings, even the words we consider holy, so that we cannot encapsulate the Christian religion in a single statement of "correct" belief, what is left? When creeds, catechisms, and articles of faith are acknowledged to be flawed efforts to say what cannot be said, mere attempts to comprehend what cannot be understood, is there a Christian religion left?

When we ask the question, "In what are we to believe?" what we are usually asking is: "In what *words* are we to believe?" But a careful reading of the Bible shows that this is the wrong question. All words are human creations. Claiming that human words and thoughts capture the divine is idolatry. The struggle against idolatry is age-old. As early as the story of the golden calf in Exodus the Bible records the continuing fight against our predilection to worship our own creations.

This is not to say that religious words and symbols are not meaningful or valuable. Nor is it to say that traditional beliefs, such as acceptance of the Bible's miracle stories, are wrong. It is not a question of right or wrong. On ultimate questions about God and about ultimate reality we are all like the blind men describing the elephant.

We must always be aware of the danger of arrogant certainty, the kind of certainty that leads to denigration, disparagement, and condemnation of those who believe differently. If we follow the way taught by Jesus, the test of beliefs is not whether they are right or wrong as factual statements, but whether they lead us to right relationship, which, in its highest form, is exemplified in love of neighbor.

If we take seriously the biblical injunction against idolatry, if we take seriously the repeated biblical warnings that God is beyond our comprehension, if we take seriously the example of Jesus' life, if we take seriously the *way* of being in the world taught and demonstrated by Jesus, we should not be asking, "What words are we to believe?" Instead we should be asking, "What way should we live?"

Micah asked: "What does the LORD require of you?" The answer was not what to believe. It was: "To *do* justice, and to *love* kindness, and to *walk humbly* with your God" (Micah 6:8). And note the words: "with *your* God." Wasn't Micah acknowledging that each of us has an image of God, and that it is just that—our own necessarily partial image?

Eternity

The present will last for us as long as we are conscious. In that sense it is our eternity. Even memories and thoughts about the future occur only in the now. Søren Kierkegaard mused that the present is the "great riddle of living in eternity, and yet hearing the hall clock strike."[14]

Although the present is eternal, our time to experience it is limited. At each moment it is up to us to make our irreplaceable store of hours into that state Jesus called the kingdom of God.

Jesus' way of being in the world is not about the future. It is about changing the nature of our priceless experience of the present. The experience of love, compassion, empathy, and kindness can only occur in the present; and this means that at every instant the "kingdom within" is within our grasp.

Love never ends.
But as for prophecies, they will come to an end;

as for tongues, they will cease;
as for knowledge, it will come to an end.

                              ∼ 1 Corinthians 13:8

Jesus taught that to live the abundant life, we must be-come free from the prison of worry about the future. We must live as little children live, in the present, open to the wonder of our existence, and without fear.

Truly I tell you, whoever does not receive the kingdom of God as a little child will never enter it.

                                     ∼ Mark 10:15

So do not worry about tomorrow, for tomorrow will bring worries of its own.

                                  ∼ Matthew 6:34

He said to his disciples, "Therefore I tell you, do not worry about your life, what you will eat, or about your body, what you will wear. For life is more than food, and the body more than clothing. Consider the ravens: they neither sow nor reap, they have neither storehouse nor barn, and yet God feeds them. Of how much more value are you than the birds!

"And can any of you by worrying add a single hour to your span of life? If then you are not able to do so small a thing as that, why do you worry about the rest?

"Consider the lilies, how they grow: they neither toil nor spin; yet I tell you, even Solomon in all his glory was not clothed like one of these. But if God so clothes the grass of the field, which is alive today and tomorrow is thrown into the oven, how much more will he clothe you—you of little faith! And do not keep striving for what you are to eat and what you are to drink, and do not keep worrying."

∼ Luke 12:22–29

Books written about being in the present make it seem difficult to accomplish. But usually when we are fully engaged in some action or some work, even if our work involves accomplishing a future goal, we are in the present. I work on tasks intended to achieve something in the future, but in the work itself, while concentrating on the task at hand, I may be completely engaged in the present. The same is true when I am giving a game my full attention. The power of games to engage us completely is one of their great gifts.

The decisive issue is not how to be in the present, it is how to change the character of the present. Zen and other forms of meditation may awaken us to the moment, but do they make today the experience of the kingdom of God? Jesus claimed that his way of love would do that, and if that is true, each day offers incalculable potential that we too often waste. G. K. Chesterton's poem "Evening" expresses the value of a single day:

Here dies another day
During which I have had eyes, ears, hands
And the great world round me;
And with tomorrow begins another.
Why am I allowed two?[15]

When we start to think about the future, anxiety often creeps in. If we use today to worry about tomorrow, fear robs us of the joy of life that could be ours this day, this moment. Look again at Jesus' statements about living in the present; they are about quelling fear and anxiety. And fear takes the joy out of life.

There are certainly many things to fear: failure, loss of love, sickness, the judgment of others, financial setback, death, loss of prestige or reputation, harm to those we love. We may think it is necessary to worry in order to take steps to avoid bad things from happening. But we can take measures to safeguard ourselves and our companions without living in fear.

Jesus' story about using talents (Matthew 25:14–28) is about fear. Before going on a journey, the master gave talents (a large sum of money) to three servants. One servant hid the talents because he was afraid of losing the money and of the master's future anger. The other two servants were not paralyzed by fear. They invested and returned a profit. When the master arrived home the first servant returned the money. The master responded: "Throw that worthless servant outside, into the darkness, where there will be weeping and gnashing of teeth."

The story is harsh. It does not suggest any sympathy for the fearful servant, and given Jesus' teachings about forgiveness and compassion, this is puzzling. But the story is a dramatic warning of the harsh consequences of fear. Each moment that our fear keeps us from experiencing the kingdom is a day we spend in the darkness, a day that cannot be recovered.

If we can overcome fear of the future there is joy to be found in the present.

> *On this day the Lord has acted;*
> *we will rejoice and be glad in it.*
>
> ⟿ Psalm 118:24

Another common barrier to experiencing the kingdom is wanting. When we spend our time wanting something we do not have, our attention is diverted from the gifts of the present. We are creatures of time; we are, literally, living time. We cannot stop time. But we must not poison the gift of this hour with desire for what we do not have.

> *The LORD is my shepherd;*
> *I shall not be in want.*
>
> ⟿ Psalm 23:1

> *You shall not covet your neighbor's house; you shall*
> *not covet your neighbor's wife, or male or female*
> *slave, or ox, or donkey, or anything that belongs to*
> *your neighbor.*
>
> ⟿ Exodus 20:17

Our culture creates desires for status and for material goods. We are constantly bombarded with advertisements. We receive messages from well-meaning family, friends, and teachers who tell us in direct and indirect ways that happiness will come with future achievement and greater possessions: from that degree from a prestigious school; from acceptance in the right social and business circles; from financial security.

My circle of friends and clients includes a number of wealthy adults who lived in very modest circumstances when they were children. None of them say that they have experienced more daily joy as adults than they experienced as children. For some the opposite has happened. They are so focused on preserving and increasing wealth that anxiety is a feature of daily life.

To change the nature of our present we must also vanquish resentment and regret about the past. According to the wisdom of the Bible, the key to preventing the past from harming us is forgiveness. Forgiving is always about something in the past, whether years past or minutes ago.

I have a cousin who feels she was wronged by her brother in the handling of their father's estate. She cannot think of her brother without upsetting herself. When her daughter married she did not invite her brother to the wedding, although, pointedly, his children were invited. On that wedding day her brother's absence was constantly in her mind. She knows that her inability to put this behind her is hurting her more that anyone, but she cannot let go of her anger.

Studies have shown that forgiving people have fewer illnesses and report greater life satisfaction. This should not surprise us, since this and other venerable lessons on the art of living would not have survived if they were not valid. The Bible insists on forgiveness:

Peter came and said to him, "Lord, if my brother sins against me, how often should I forgive? As many as seven times? Jesus said to him, "Not seven times, but, I tell you, seventy times seven."

~ Matthew 18:21–22

You shall not take vengeance or bear a grudge against any of your people, but you shall love your neighbor as yourself.

~ Leviticus 19:18

For I will forgive their iniquity, and remember their sin no more.

~ Jeremiah 31:34

Blessed are the merciful, for they will receive mercy.

~ Matthew 5:7

Bear with one another and, if anyone has a complaint against another, forgive each other; just as the Lord has forgiven you, so you also must forgive.

~ Colossians 3:13

For if you forgive others their trespasses, your heavenly Father will also forgive you.

~ Matthew 6:14

> *But I say to those that listen, Love your enemies, do*
> *good to those who hate you, bless those who curse*
> *you, pray for those who abuse you. If anyone strikes*
> *you on the cheek, offer the other also.*
>
> ⁓ Luke 6:27–29

In speaking of forgiveness we return again to the magic of love because forgiveness is another aspect of loving-kindness. It rests on a willingness to overcome our hurt feelings, our pride, our need for revenge, and to replace those feelings with compassion.

Jesus' teachings are not mere techniques for living in the moment. They are intended to give the "now" a better, deeper, greater quality. They are the keys to entering what Jesus called the kingdom of God, and doing so in this life.

Much has been written about the importance of living in the present. For centuries many Zen practitioners have been taught to spend years learning how to engage in deep meditation in order to become awake to the present. The time and intense training required shows us that this level of consciousness is extremely difficult to attain. The reason is apparent to anyone who has tried to do so by meditation alone—our minds continually fight our attempts to be centered on the present, and carry us into the past and the future. Although the present is always with us, it is un-graspable, and our thoughts run away with us, calling us to think of future rewards, to want something we do not have now, or to think about the past.

Consciously and unconsciously we learn ways to overcome the anxiety and discomfort that often come with thoughts of the future or the past. Reading an absorbing murder mystery or getting lost in a movie are familiar and pleasant pastimes.

Jesus' way is not escapist. Nor is his way of waking up to the present self-centered. It does not separate us from the people around us. His way requires conscious engagement with family, friends, acquaintances, and strangers.

We do not experience the true richness of the *kingdom of God* by escaping into a novel, a movie, or a meditative trance, although these activities have their own rewards. The promise of the Bible is that we can do better. When Jesus taught that we should take no thought for the morrow, he was talking about something more than defeating worry about the future. Jesus was talking about recreating the present. His *way* goes beyond merely becoming aware of the "now" to a singular way of being in it. His message was and is that we can change the present into the kingdom of God by being a person of love.

The world in which we live is relational, and when we change our relation with it, we change our world. Physicists, such as Heisenberg, Bohm, Bohr, Einstein, Feynman, and Schrödinger, have shown that there is no ultimate, solid, material reality, only relationships of relationships. But long before modern physics, both the Old and New Testaments taught that the penultimate way to live this life is to live in loving relationship.

*"You shall love the Lord your God with all your heart,
and with all your soul, and with all your mind." This
is the greatest and first commandment. And a second
is like it: "You shall love your neighbor as yourself."*
                                        ∼ Matthew 22:37–39

We have read that "God is love" (1 John 4:8). Although
this sounds like a definition, it is not. It is a description of
the experience of the kingdom of God.

Although it transforms the present, loving-kindness
does not depart from it or ignore it. When we use the present moment to care for someone else, to be a friend, we
are not only fully in the present, we change it into the
kingdom.

We often think of ourselves as isolated entities, but we
are actually a part of a network of physical and emotional
relationships. Each of us is a dependent part of numerous
interrelated dynamic systems. The air we breathe, the
water we drink, and the food we eat moves into us and
through us. If any of them stop for a significant time we
die. Commercial relationships provide us with food and
shelter. Without fulfilling emotional relationships with
others we wither as surely as a plant that is not watered.
When a marriage or an important friendship is changed,
whether for the better or the worse, we change with it.
Who hasn't had a day brightened or spoiled as the result
of a change in a relationship?

Making compassion the foundation of our relationships is not only the cornerstone of Christ's ministry, it has

been recognized by wisdom figures in every tradition. When asked to state the essence of Buddhism, the Dalai Lama replied: "My religion is compassion." The Vedas and the Upanishads teach that there is an unbreakable bond between our degree of compassion and our karma, that is, between the way we relate to the world and the others in it and our experience in life. The Hindu philosopher Eknath Easwaran entitled one of his books about the Bhagavad Gita *To Love Is to Know Me*. In it he says if we begin living "as the Buddha lived—'for the welfare of all, for the joy of all'—... then the Buddha, the Christ, comes to life in us."[16]

The fact that we are an assembly of relationships explains why it is true that when we change the character of our relationships we change both ourselves and the world in which we live. If we infuse ourselves with anxiety or anger, we condemn ourselves to a certain type of life. To love, to be compassionate, to be forgiving, to be kind, is to create a new way of life. In it we transcend our self-absorption and recreate our world.

There are many levels and kinds of love. On one level, there is simple courtesy and friendliness. At a higher level there is generosity, empathy, and compassion. There is love of those who return our love; and for those who are capable of it, there is love of enemies.

You have heard that it was said, "You shall love your neighbor and hate your enemy." But I say to you, Love your enemies and pray for those who persecute you.
∼ Matthew 5:43–44

Jesus led a life that was so loving that he asked for forgiveness for his torturers while he was dying on the cross.

Father, forgive them; for they do not know what they are doing.
∼ Luke 23:34

Most of us have known people who, to some degree, at some time or times in their lives, have lived the way of loving-kindness. They come from all faiths and no faith, from all walks of life. They are atheists, Unitarians, Mormons, Baptists, agnostics, evangelicals, Jews, Episcopalians, Catholics, Buddhists, liberals and conservatives, Republicans and Democrats, teachers and laborers.

It is easy to fall into the trap of thinking that the "real" Christians are people who share our beliefs. But if living the commandment to love our neighbor is the essence of Jesus' ministry, then anyone who lives a life of love can be said to be a follower of Jesus' way, and thus "Christian."

Of course, this usage of the term "Christian" conflicts with the understanding of many that to be a Christian you must believe the creedal statements are factually true. But who follows Jesus' way more closely: a non-believer who lives a life of compassion, or the believer who has little or no compassion for others?

I recall a conversation years ago with one of my law partners who is Jewish. He had spent months providing free legal services to a woman he barely knew. The paperwork to successfully conclude her legal problem had been completed a few minutes before we were to leave for a short trip. As we got into his car he was smiling and I asked why. He explained that he had just been told that he was "a good Christian man." He thought it ironic. I think it was accurate.

One of my neighbors is on a different place in the belief spectrum from my law partner. He is a traditional conservative Christian. He firmly believes that the accounts of Jesus' miracles in the New Testament are factually true. He is also a "good Christian man," because I know the generous and compassionate way of life he leads.

The Christianity that we discover by doing what Jesus taught us to do leads to some different conclusions about religion than does the focus on belief. Propositional belief is not the *way* taught by Jesus. One may believe Jesus returned from death and still fail to love one's neighbors. One may adamantly reject that belief and live in love.

If, as Jesus taught, the two greatest commandments of the Judeo-Christian tradition require that we infuse ourselves with a loving spirit, it must follow that "correct belief" in the traditional sense of that phrase is simply irrelevant.

They are to do good, to be rich in good works,
generous, and ready to share, thus storing up for

themselves the treasure of a good foundation for the future, so that they may take hold of the life that really is life.

∽ 1 Timothy 6:18–19

Let us love, not in word or speech, but in truth and action.

∽ 1 John 3:18

Everyone who loves is born of God and knows God.

∽ 1 John 4:7

Those who abide in love abide in God, and God abides in them.

∽ 1 John 4:16

Paul said it unmistakably. Belief is not decisive, only love is.

If I have all faith, so as to remove mountains, but do not have love, I am nothing.

∽ 1 Corinthians 13:2

∼ 9 ∼

What Am I Willing to Do?

You and I face two questions: Is Jesus' *way* of doing life a better way of living this life? Are we willing to act on the claim that it is? But these actually coalesce into a single question, because in this age most of us are empiricists, which means that for us there is only one acceptable method of answering the first question, and that is see if it works by trying it. But to try Jesus' way is daunting. It asks us:

∼ To try to give up the attempt to find the abundant life through knowledge. The "kingdom within" isn't found through understanding. The kingdom of God is found through loving-kindness.

∼ To try to give up worry and fear. Worry and fear are almost always about the future. Death is always in the future. We can plan for the future, even for death, without becoming fearful. By overcoming anxiety

about the future we lift its burden and allow ourselves the opportunity to experience the present in all
its richness. "So do not worry about tomorrow, for
tomorrow will bring worries of its own" (Matthew
6:34).

~ To try to give up anger, regret, and sorrow
about the past. By forgiveness of ourselves and others
we break free of the chains of the past. "Lord, if my
brother sins against me, how often should I forgive?
As many as seven times?" Jesus replied: "Not seven
times, but, I tell you, seventy times seven" (Matthew
18:21–22).

~ To try to refuse to spoil the irreplaceable pres-
ent moment by wanting something we do not have.
"The LORD is my shepherd; I shall not be in want"
(Psalm 23). "You shall not covet" (Exodus 20:17).

We know that we cannot completely defeat worry. We
cannot always forgive. We cannot eliminate all desire for
what we do not have. We cannot even continuously remember to try to do these things. Helpfully, Paul had a
talent for reducing all commandments, all laws, to the one
essential:

*Owe no one anything, except to love one another; for
the one who loves another has fulfilled the law. The
commandments, "You shall not commit adultery; You
shall not murder; You shall not steal; You shall not
covet"; and any other commandment, are summed up*

in this word, "Love your neighbor as yourself." Love
does no wrong to a neighbor; therefore, love is the
fulfilling of the law.

           ~ Romans 13:8–10

In his first letter to the Corinthians Paul again summed
up the essence of this Christianity:

If I speak in the tongues of mortals and of angels, but
do not have love, I am a noisy gong or a clanging
cymbal. And if I have prophetic powers, and
understand all mysteries and all knowledge, and if I
have all faith, so as to remove mountains, but do not
have love, I am nothing. If I give away all my
possessions, and if I hand over my body so that I may
boast, but do not have love, I gain nothing.

Love is patient; love is kind; love is not envious or
boastful or arrogant or rude. It does not insist on its
own way; it is not irritable or resentful; it does not
rejoice in wrongdoing, but rejoices in the truth. It
bears all things, believes all things, hopes all things,
endures all things.

Love never ends. But as for prophecies, they will come
to an end; as for tongues, they will cease; as for
knowledge, it will come to an end. . . .

And now faith, hope, and love abide, these three; and
the greatest of these is love.

           ~ I Corinthians 13:1–13

This sounds simple enough, but changing our habitual, daily attitude is an immense task. Any psychologist, psychiatrist, or twelve-step counselor will tell us that. Changing a mindset, an outlook, a psychological set point, requires consistent daily action over an extended period of time.

But as difficult as it may be to make these changes, it is possible. There are people who have succeeded and we can look to them for guidance. Over the centuries monastics have developed practices to accomplish interior change. One of the most well-known and established Christian orders is the Benedictine.

The *Rule of Saint Benedict,* written in the middle of the sixth century, prescribes these activities, *repeated daily:*

- seven services of prayer;

- the "lesser silence" during the day, and the "greater silence" at night;

- *lectio divina,* the slow, purposeful study of the Bible; and

- performing good works—acts of altruism and compassion.

Benedict exhorted his monks to be cheerful and mutually supportive. The two central elements of this life are prayer (a form of meditation), and maintaining a spirit of loving-kindness.

These activities are meant to occur in a community. Benedict recognized that we usually cannot accomplish significant change by acting alone. We know from our own experience that we will probably not continue any new activity unless we have support from others.

Groups influence our states of mental and physical health, for good or ill. We seek out groups where we will be accepted. Acceptance itself is a form of loving-kindness and the importance of finding a supportive community cannot be overstated. Many churches and temples offer caring communities. This is a reason why many are drawn to religious organizations despite not believing everything that is said there.

One of the principal factors accounting for the remarkable growth of evangelical churches is their emphasis on the formation of supportive subgroups and consequent constant attention to the creation and maintenance of numerous venues for personal interaction through sports leagues, Bible studies, young married groups, seniors groups, Sunday school, Wednesday night suppers, and youth trips. The declining mainstream denominations seem largely oblivious to the fact that the common foundation of all successful churches, regardless of differences in beliefs, is the establishment and maintenance of supportive small groups where friendships can form in a caring atmosphere.

When I was in college, and not attending any church, on a visit home I asked my father why I should bother attending church when I didn't believe much that was as-

serted there. He answered that in church I would find people I would want to be a part of my life. Looking back on
that answer, given decades ago, I realize that it wisely priv-
ileged relationship over belief.

The relationships I have with people I know through
my church have meant much to me, and many of them
have a different quality from those formed through business or social contacts. It is hard to put my finger on just
how they are different. Part of the difference may come
from a shared sense that we need to be supportive of one
another, or from the sense of knowing that we have similar
values. Part of the difference may result from simply being
in contact on a regular basis with the same people for
many years.

Those relationships were not formed by simply attending services and listening to sermons. They grew from attending Sunday school classes and participating in church
suppers, from engaging in retreats, fundraising projects,
and trips with youth, from delivering and receiving meals
or flowers in times of illness or in times of mourning. I am
aware of the importance of having participated in the life
of a particular congregation, and of the value of friendships formed in the context of a religious community in
which I have shared the events of life—mundane, joyful,
and tragic. Differing propositional beliefs are irrelevant to
these friendships.

Saint Benedict taught that we should remind ourselves
each morning that we are going to die. He did not say that
to make us fearful. He said it because we tend to sleepwalk

through life. We need to wake up and make the gift of each day count. How much of today was spent in creating or nurturing compassionate relationships with those around us? What did I do with the irreplaceable time I was given today?

We really do *spend* our time. Time is our ultimate currency, and each day we draw down from an ever-reduced store. Our time is literally priceless. How careful, how thoughtful, how intentional are we about how, and with whom, we spend our time? Are we as careful with it as we are with our money?

The pattern of daily monastic life was developed over centuries, and it reflects an effort to make time meaningful. Despite different beliefs, monks and nuns worldwide have established similar practices. When the Cistercian monk Thomas Merton became a resident guest in a Buddhist monastery in Japan he was stuck by the similarity of the practices of the two traditions. The explanation must be that, although the two had different beliefs and were isolated from each other, over the centuries those practices that were worthwhile were retained and those of little worth were discarded.

Will some monastic practices better our lives? Will they help us make better use of our time? The only way to discover the answer to that question is to try them. Perhaps we will be more inclined to experiment if we know the results of recent studies.

The tools of contemporary medicine, such as electroencephalography, magnetic resonance imaging, and blood chemistry studies, have been used to study Christian and Buddhist monastics engaged in the long-term practice of loving-kindness meditation. The studies have shown that daily meditation or prayer, especially with thoughts of compassion, if practiced regularly over an extended period of time, will increase blood flow, growth, and electrical activity in the left prefrontal cortex, a part of the brain associated with happiness and states of well being, as well as with analytic thinking. Maintaining loving thoughts also increases levels of serotonin, a natural chemical that tends to reduce anxiety and increase calmness.[17]

There are Tibetan and Indian Buddhists monks who are trained to inculcate loving-kindness into their way of life though a three-thousand-year-old meditation known in the Pali language as the Metta Bhavana. When monks who had practiced it for years were studied by EEG and MRI, it was discovered that this meditation produced "off the chart" gamma waves in the left prefrontal cortex.

Recently the brains of Carmelite nuns have been studied with EEG and MRI while they were engaged in centering prayer. The results were similar to those observed in Tibetan monks engaged in the loving-kindness meditation. The researchers reported that the monks and nuns who participated in the studies were unusually kind and happy.[18]

Prayer, of course, may be dismissed by skeptics who do not believe there is a God, or who do not believe we could communicate with God even if that God exists. But, as someone wise once said, prayer isn't intended to change God, it is intended to change us. Here a variation of Metta Bhavana adapted to become prayer.

Sit quietly. Take a few deep breaths. Start by praying for loving-kindness for yourself. Then pray that others will experience loving-kindness by saying:

"May _____ be happy, may _____ experience love, may _____ experience peace."

Begin with a prayer for a loved one; then for a friend; then for a respected mentor or wisdom figure; then for a person for whom you have neutral feelings; progressing to a person for whom you have negative feelings; all people; all conscious beings; and the universe. Sometimes words can distract from generating feelings of loving-kindness. The words can be replaced by simply thinking of the subjects, perhaps picturing them, while attempting to "send" loving-kindness to them.

Jim Coleman, now a retired Episcopal bishop, was my wife's boss for several years. He is one of those people who is a pleasure to be with. When Robbie was working for him she learned that every night he prayed, by name, for his family, for his staff, for his staff's family, and for a long list of others. Although he would not have used that term, he was performing Metta Bhavana.

The brain is an organ designed to adapt and change. Contrary to the assumptions made for many years, it is now known that new growth can be accomplished even in older brains. Thus, regular periods of focused concentration in meditation are now being prescribed to fight dementia.

There are, of course, many ways to meditate. However, only focused, concentrated periods of meditation will have a measurable effect on the brain. Methods such as praying the rosary and centering prayer require focused concentration. Reading the Bible slowly and praying or meditating on what is read, a traditional practice known as *lectio divina,* requires similar concentration.

My father-in-law practiced *lectio divina,* although as far as I know he never heard the term. He was a chemical engineer, a fisherman, a duck hunter, an avid golfer, a pilot in World War II. He did not appear to be a particularly religious man. But during a visit with him near the end of his life I learned that he had the lifelong habit of beginning each day in quiet, reading the Bible. He started on page one, methodically read through to the end, then started again. Whether it was the result of genetics, or this practice, or both, he was mentally sharp until the day he died at age 92.

My maternal grandmother also followed the practice of daily Bible reading. She had a difficult life marked by illness and times of poverty. She was the victim of spousal abuse and, as a result, she eventually became a single mother raising three children during the Great Depression. But she had a loving engagement with the world that came from having been daily immersed in her Bible and in the support of her church-going small-town community.

A method of prayer called centering prayer has been written about by the Christian monks Thomas Keating and Basil Pennington. Here is an adaptation of this form of prayer, using traditional images:

> Sit comfortably with your eyes closed. Relax, and quiet yourself. Feel the love of God. Choose a few sacred words that best express your intention to be in the Lord's presence and open to God's loving action within you, words such as "Christ be within me," "Come, Lord Jesus," "Come, Holy Spirit." Let this intention be gently present as your symbol of your sincere intention to be open to, and a vehicle of, God's loving action within you. Whenever you become aware of thoughts or feelings that distract you, simply return to your sacred words.

Maintaining an interior state of loving-kindness is a constant in these practices. It should not surprise us to learn that Christians, steeped in the importance of love, have developed numerous methods for the maintenance of a compassionate state.

There is an ancient tradition, reflected in the writings of the Desert Fathers (ca. 200–400), the Cistercian monk Bernard of Clairvaux (ca. 1090–1153), Meister Eckhart (ca. 1260–1328), and others, of continually thinking of

"Christ within me" to create a state of being in which each of us becomes a medium for the transmission of love.

Brother Lawrence, a seventeenth-century French monk, practiced the presence of God constantly as he worked in the monastery kitchen. Letters and conversations about his practice were preserved and have been published as a book entitled *The Practice of the Presence of God*. In one of his letters he writes:

> I have ceased all forms of devotion and set prayers except those which my state requires. I make it my priority to persevere in His holy presence, wherein I maintain a simple attention and a fond regard for God, which I may call an actual presence of God. Or, to put it another way, it is an habitual, silent, and private conversation of the soul with God. This gives me much joy and contentment. In short, I am sure, beyond all doubt, that my soul has been with God above these past thirty years.[19]

In Ireland, Saint Patrick (ca. 390–460) wrote a series of verses that have come to be known as Saint Patrick's Breastplate. It is a prayer asking for protection and to be a conduit of Christ-like love. Many versions and adaptations of the prayer have been developed over the centuries, such as this one.

> I arise today
> With the power of heaven
> Under the sun in splendor,

Christ within me:
Christ before me,
Christ behind me,
Christ at my right hand,
Christ at my left,
Christ below and Christ above,
Christ in every ear that hears me,
Christ in every hand that touches me,
Christ in every eye that sees me,
Christ in every heart that thinks of me.[20]

Infusing oneself with love is central to all of these practices. Whether we think of them as techniques to change our dendrites, or we prefer to say that we are seeking the "kingdom of God within," the goal is the same: to thoroughly incorporate loving-kindness into our daily lives.

Seeking this goal does not require becoming a monk or a nun. Nor does it require thousands of hours of practice before we begin to experience the effects of such practices. One study showed that after only two weeks of loving-kindness meditation for thirty minutes a day there are measurable increases in activity levels in the left prefrontal cortex, the area, as we have noted, associated with happiness. I have not come across any EEG study of the effect of being kind to everyone we see today, but many of us can confirm from personal experience that the effects of that practice are immediate.

It is well documented that there is a strong correlation between altruism and happiness.[21] For twenty years I practiced law with a man who was decades older than I. On more than one occasion I walked to the courthouse with him. Our route took us through a city park often occupied by people asking for a handout. My partner always gave some money to anyone who asked. One day he saw the question in my eyes. He said: "They are doing me a favor." Years later, after I tried that practice myself, I understood his statement.

As I write this I think about a television preacher who says to his audience that if they are "faithful" (I think that means if they believe the right things and if they send his church money), God will reward them with a "payday." He promises such things as promotions at work and financial windfalls: things that are in the future. I don't believe that sending this preacher a check will produce a windfall. But I know from my own experience that doing something good for someone else today will, in fact, produce a "payday"—a welcome interior change in me.

We know that patterns of thought make us who we are. In *Paradise Lost,* John Milton wrote, "The mind is its own place, and in itself can make a heaven of hell or a hell of heaven." This truth is also reflected in the teachings of the Bible. Paul's letter to the Philippians shows that he had the same insight:

> *Finally, beloved, whatever is true, whatever is*
> *honorable, whatever is just, whatever is pure,*
> *whatever is pleasing, whatever is commendable, if*
> *there is any excellence and if there is anything worthy*

of praise, think about these things. Keep on doing the
things that you have learned and received and heard
and seen in me, and the God of peace will be with you.
                                    ～ Philippians 4:8–9

Out of inanimate matter we have been brought to life
and somehow provided with nerves, cells, consciousness,
and the tools necessary to create that state of being which
Jesus called "the kingdom of God within." We are, in the
words of Psalm 139, "wonderfully made." These are gifts,
as the universe is a gift. For a great many people science
defines their understanding of existence. But science cannot tell us the ultimate source of these gifts or why we have
been given them. And we do not need to know. We only
need to know how to create abundant life.

∿ 10 ∿

Death

I am at an age when many people I loved have died. I have far fewer years left than the years I have already spent. Is there life after death? In the most realistic dream I have ever had, my father, dead for a year, stood beside my bed and told me that I should not fear death.

I find it extremely difficult to believe this experience was anything other than a dream, or to believe that after death I will exist, or feel again the presence of my mother, father, grandmothers, aunts, and uncles, or know again the friendship of those I have lost. But on what evidence should I conclude that death leads to nothingness?

As the world becomes more secular, the assumption that death leads to nothingness is increasingly widespread. Yet I cannot know anything about myself after death. As Epictetus pointed out, if death is nothingness, when I am dead I will not experience it. If I think of death as a continuation of existence in another form, nothing in my experience tells me what that form would look like. As we move inevitably toward death we are in relation to something beyond us, so far removed from our experience, so foreign, that it is unthinkable—unimaginable. One thing we all have in common is the fact that we will die, but our own deaths, and the deaths of our companions, are wholly, utterly, absolutely, unknowable.

Death isn't a matter of knowledge. It cannot be. I know nothing of what happens after death. Nor do I know anything about the unknown cause-without-a-cause that both cannot be and must be, which set off and continues the chain of events that, after billions of years, brought me into life. Yet I was somehow brought into existence. As I go about my days I demonstrate my unconscious faith in the mystery with every breath. The question of death is only one of many questions I cannot answer. But my inability to answer questions about the universe, about how and why reality came to be does not prevent reality from existing. Shouldn't I trust this mystery about death?

I take comfort in the fact that reality, the ground of being, the first cause, God by whatever name, is ultimately beyond my comprehension. The undeniable fact of this great enigma puts the lie to the religion of materialism and its assumption that nothing exists that is beyond our comprehension. Even if I cannot convince myself that Jesus returned from the dead I know that there is—and this is my certainty—a reality beyond our ability to comprehend.

That reality that transcends what "I" can know brought me into being, keeps me alive, and will carry "me" into death. I have the habit of thinking of myself as separate and apart from reality. But that image is an illusion. "I" am not separate and apart. I am a part of reality.

Are my parents and friends waiting for me in an afterlife? The ideas, the words, the images I believe or do not believe about death will not make it so or not so. What may happen to me when "I" die is not knowable by me. The only thing I can experience now is this life.

> *Jesus said: "And as for the resurrection of the dead,*
> *have you not read what was said to you by God, 'I am*
> *the God of Abraham, the God of Isaac, and the God of*
> *Jacob'? He is God not of the dead, but of the living."*
> *And when the crowd heard it, they were astounded at*
> *his teaching.*
>
>   ∼ Matthew 22:31–33

The philosophy of materialism may make life and death appear to be pointless; but when it does so it is blind to its own blindness. Every philosophy is a creation of the human mind, a limited model of an impenetrable mystery that surrounds and constitutes our lives and our deaths. The fact that we cannot comprehend the unknown does not prevent it from being real. "Reality is by no means exhausted by the concepts in which we mediate it; put theologically, 'God' is not a pure construct of our language."[22]

We cannot know the unknown. Given the limitless depth and breadth of what we do not know, the poetry of the church is, for me, a better way to speak of its reality. The burial service of the *Book of Common Prayer,* quoting Romans 14:8, says it well:

For if we have life, we are alive in the Lord,
and if we die, we die in the Lord.
So, then, whether we live or die,
we are the Lord's possession.[23]

To believe is to accept a proposition as true. Propositions are made of words or numbers or both, and words and numbers are symbols of our thoughts. Our thoughts cannot encompass this limitless mystery in which we find ourselves—which some of us call God.

All we have are metaphors. This is why, although I do not believe in the literal truth of the creeds, I can attend an Easter service and sing: "'Welcome happy morning!'...Lo! The dead is living, God for evermore!" I sing as life made of the inert detritus of exploded stars. I sing as a part of this transcendent mystery we try to name but cannot.

Conclusion

The introduction to this book contrasted two *mythos:* that of traditional, institutional Christianity, which offers an image of God that has human characteristics, and that of scientific materialism, which offers an ultimately meaningless universe.

The images and language historically offered by Christianity, when presented as factual descriptions of reality, no longer ring true. The common images and language of scientific materialism are those of mathematics and they do ring true, but only in describing the quantifiable.

As we have seen, no language, no image, no description, is the same as the reality it attempts to describe. This endless mystery in which we live and move and have our being exceeds our ideas and language. The transcendent, the beyond, is not far away, it is part and parcel of every breath and every moment, if we will only be aware.

Where does that leave us? I suggest that it leaves us with our focus not on beliefs, but on how to create that interior state of compassion and selflessness that Jesus called the kingdom of God.

You may not agree that one can follow Jesus and thus be "Christian" without believing that the statements made in the church's creeds are factually true. You may not agree that Christianity ought not to be about belief in creeds and should only be about living Jesus' *way*. Even so, if you are familiar with the New Testament I think you will agree, whether you are a religious liberal, a religious conservative, or non-religious, that Jesus' central message was and is that we should make ourselves into people of loving-kindness.

"Getting and spending, we lay waste our powers," Wordsworth said so well. We know that even possession of immense wealth will not fulfill our lives. To the contrary, materialism leads to meaninglessness.

> *It is easier for a camel to go through the eye of a*
> *needle than for someone who is rich to enter the*
> *kingdom of God.*
>
> ~ Matthew 19:24

In our culture we tend to assume that the linkage between our wealth and our happiness is unbreakable. But ancient biblical wisdom asserts that, regardless of the state of our finances, living in love will change our lives into something richer.

Jesus taught that if we maintain a spirit of loving-kindness we will experience a more abundant life. He taught that "the kingdom of God is within you" (Luke 17:21). His disciples told us that "there is no fear in love" (1 John 4:18). His theologians tell us that in love we touch "the beyond in the midst of life."[24]

Our own experience has shown us that in the times we have been filled with love our world was altered. But recalling those times is not enough. Merely accepting as true that love will change our world is not enough. Planning to be kind later is not enough.

Believing, being convinced, even possessing absolute certainty that love is the key to the kingdom is not *loving*. No matter how strong my desire for the abundant life, I cannot have it unless I make this internal change.

We have heard that hours of prayer and meditation will change our lives for the better, but if we cannot, or will not, spend hours in prayer or meditation, we need to recall that the goal is not meditation or prayer; it is to become persons of loving-kindness. We can do that by daily reminding ourselves to think thoughts of compassion and to perform acts of kindness. We can do that all day, every day, ultimately for thousands of hours, regardless of the other demands on our time.

Jesus taught that the two greatest commandments amount to the same thing:

> *And a second is like it: "You shall love your neighbor as yourself."*
>
> ∽ Matthew 22:39

According to Jesus, "loving" is the law of the Lord. Psalm 1 tells us:

Blessed are those whose delight
*   is in the law of the LORD,*
and on his law they meditate day and night.
They are like trees planted by streams of water,
*   which yield their fruit in its season,*
and their leaves do not wither.

~ Psalm 1:1–3

We know that at every second of consciousness we have some attitude, some outlook, through which we encounter and interact with the world. Whatever our mood is, that mood shapes and colors each moment, each thought, each action. And we know from our own experience that when we change our internal attitude we change the world we live in.

When we say "I believe that this is the case," we express a conclusion about a proposition that can be doubted. For example, I may say, "I believe that Jesus walked on water," or, "I believe that my scientific theory is true." The expression of an idea in this form confirms that it may be doubted.

But there is a realm in which doubt is not a factor. Experiences we live are that realm. They are in a different category from things we believe.

I say, "I am alive."
    I don't say, "I believe I am alive."

I say, "I am seeing."
    I don't say "I think I am seeing."

I say, "I am breathing."
    I don't say, "I believe I am breathing."

In experiencing we are not involved with propositions, with words, with theories.

What would our experience of the world be like if it were the experience of loving? A hypothetical answer has no validity. The only meaningful answer to this question is the one we find through our own experience.

What if it is true? What if living the way of love is the way, the only way to the "pearl beyond price," to the "kingdom of God" to be found within us? I say this to myself above all: What if it is true and I miss it because I didn't really try?

Endnotes

1. *Mishkan T'filah: A Reform Siddur,* ed. Elyse D. Frishman (New York: Central Conference of American Rabbis Press, 2007), 171. The entire prayer reads: "Days pass and the years vanish, and we walk sightless among miracles. God, fill our eyes with seeing and our minds with knowing; let there be moments when Your Presence, like lightning, illumines the darkness in which we walk. Help us to see, wherever we gaze, that the bush burns unconsumed. And we, clay touched by God, will reach out for holiness, and exclaim in wonder, How filled with awe is this place, and we did not know it!"
2. Friedrich Schleiermacher, *The Christian Faith* (London: T&T Clark, 1999; first published in 1830).
3. Jean-Luc Marion, "The Impossible for Man—God," an essay in *Transcendence and Beyond: A Postmodern Inquiry,* ed. John D. Caputo and Michael J. Scanlon (Bloomington: Indiana University Press, 2007), 25.
4. "The reading processes that we have just seen at work suggest, first, that the statement commented on exceeds what it originally wanted to say; that it contains more than it contains; that perhaps an inexhaustible surplus of meaning remains locked in the syntactic structures of the sentence, in its word-groups, its actual words, phonemes and letters, in all this

materiality of the saying which is potentially signifying all the time." Emmanuel Levinas, *Beyond the Verse: Talmudic Readings and Lectures,* trans. Gary D. Mole (London: The Althone Press, 1982, 1995), 109.

5. Albert Einstein, *Living Philosophies* (New York: Simon and Schuster, 1931), 6.

6. As quoted in Aage Petersen, "The Philosophy of Niels Bohr," *Bulletin of the Atomic Scientists* 19, no. 7 (September 1963): 8.

7. Bart D. Ehrman, *God's Problem: How the Bible Fails to Answer Our Most Important Question—Why We Suffer* (New York: HarperCollins, 2008).

8. John D. Caputo, *The Prayers and Tears of Jacques Derrida: Religion without Religion* (Bloomington: Indiana University Press, 1997), 331.

9. Ludwig Wittgenstein, *Tractatus Logico-Philosophicus,* trans. D. F. Pears and B. F. McGuinness (London: Routledge, 2001), 89.

10. For this reason Wittgenstein came to the conclusion that, except for its last statement concerning the need for silence, the *Tractatus* was misguided.

11. Raimundo Panikkar, *The Silence of God: The Answer of the Buddha* (Maryknoll, N.Y.: Orbis Books, 1989), 173.

12. David Bohm, *Wholeness and the Implicate Order* (London: Routledge, 1980), 242.

13. Denise Levertov, "Primary Wonder," in *Sands of the Well* (New York: New Directions Publishing, 1994, 1995, 1996), 129. Denise Levertov (1923–1997) was the daughter of a Russian Jew who was trained to be a rabbi and became an Anglican priest in England.

14. Søren Kierkegaard, *Either/Or,* trans. Walter Lowrie, vol. 2 (Princeton, N.J.: Princeton University Press, 1949), 89.

15. G. K. Chesterton, "Evening," in *The Collected Works of G. K. Chesterton, Volume X: Collected Poetry, Part 1,* ed. Aidan Mackey (San Francisco: Ignatius, 1994), 38.

16. Eknath Easwaran, *To Love Is to Know Me: The Bhagavad Gita for Daily Living,* vol. 3 (Petaluma, Calif.: Nilgiri Press, 1979), 161.

17. Sonja Lyubomirsky's *The How of Happiness* (New York: Penguin Books, 2007) contains thirty-four pages of endnotes citing published studies, not limited to studies of monks and nuns, that bear on the effects of practices commonly used by monastics.

18. See, for example, the research documented in Mario Beauregard and Denyse O'Leary, *The Spiritual Brain: A Neuroscientist's Case for the Existence of the Soul* (New York: HarperCollins, 2007).

19. Brother Lawrence, *The Practice of the Presence of God,* second letter, quoted from the Light Heart edition (1999-2007), www.lookingforachurch.org/uploads/PracticingGod.pdf.

20. Quoted in John McQuiston II, *A Prayer Book for the 21st Century* (Harrisburg: Morehouse Publishing, 2004), 73.

21. See, for example, Stephen G. Post, "Altruism, Happiness, and Health: It's Good to be Good," *International Journal of Behavioral Medicine* 12, no. 2 (2005): 66–77.

22. Roland Faber, *God as Poet of the World: Exploring Process Theologies* (Louisville: Westminster John Knox Press, 2008), 43.

23. *The Book of Common Prayer* (New York: Church Hymnal Corporation, 1979), 491.

24. Dietrich Bonhoeffer, *A Testament to Freedom: The Essential Writings of Dietrich Bonhoeffer,* ed. Geffrey B. Kelly and F. Burton Nelson (New York: Harper Collins, 1995), 493. I think that what I have been saying is close to what Bonhoeffer meant when he called for a "religionless Christianity."

Acknowledgments

I am at an age when what I write and think has many origins, but the influence of the liberal Episcopal and Presbyterian tradition and culture in which I was raised must be acknowledged as primary. I give greatest thanks for the influence of deceased and living family members, and I also acknowledge the influence of friends and mentors who have shared with me an interest in "religion" broadly conceived. A part of that milieu are the people of Morehouse who have chosen to publish my books, including Debra Farrington, editor of my first book, and Joan Castagnone, my present editor. To both, special thanks.